Managing Training and Development Finance

Fiona Green and Ken Langdon

- ■ Fast-track route to how effective training and development spend enhances organizational as well as individual performance and growth

- ■ Covers the importance of adopting the right mind-set to training and development investment, how to bridge the gap between training and performance, planning and allocating resources, and the bottom-line benefits

- ■ Examples and lessons from a case study of a service organization seeking to redirect the HR team and improve the HR contribution to the company, using the Return on Investment model to justify a major change project, and using interventions to ensure projects achieve their objectives

- ■ Includes a comprehensive resources guide, key concepts and thinkers, a 10-step action plan and a section of FAQs

≫EXPRESS EXEC.COM≪

essential management thinking at your fingertips

T0313457

First Published 2003 by
Capstone Publishing Limited (a Wiley company)
8 Newtec Place
Magdalen Road
Oxford OX4 1RE
United Kingdom
http://www.capstoneideas.com

CIP catalogue records for this book are available from the British Library and the US Library of Congress

ISBN 1-84112-451-6

Printed and bound in Great Britain by CPI Antony Rowe, Eastbourne

Wiley also publishes its books in a variety of electronic formats. Some content that appears in print may not be available in electronic books.

Websites often change their contents and addresses; details of sites listed in this book were accurate at the time of writing, but may change.

Substantial discounts on bulk quantities of Capstone Books are available to corporations, professional associations and other organizations. For details telephone Capstone Publishing on (+44-1865-798623), fax (+44-1865-240941) or email (info@wiley-capstone.co.uk).

Contents

Introduction to ExpressExec

ExpressExec is a completely up-to-date resource of current business practice, accessible in a number of ways – anytime, anyplace, anywhere. ExpressExec combines best practice cases, key ideas, action points, glossaries, further reading, and resources.

Each module contains 10 individual titles that cover all the key aspects of global business practice. Written by leading experts in their field, the knowledge imparted provides executives with the tools and skills to increase their personal and business effectiveness, benefiting both employee and employer.

ExpressExec is available in a number of formats:

» **Print** – 120 titles available through retailers or printed on demand using any combination of the 1200 chapters available.
» **E-Books** – e-books can be individually downloaded from ExpressExec.com or online retailers onto PCs, handheld computers, and e-readers.
» **Online** – http://www.expressexec.wiley.com/ provides fully searchable access to the complete ExpressExec resource via the Internet – a cost-effective online tool to increase business expertise across a whole organization.

» **ExpressExec Performance Support Solution (EEPSS)** – a software solution that integrates ExpressExec content with interactive tools to provide organizations with a complete internal management development solution.
» **ExpressExec Rights and Syndication** – ExpressExec content can be licensed for translation or display within intranets or on Internet sites.

To find out more visit www.ExpressExec.com or contact elound@wiley-capstone.co.uk.

Introduction to Managing Training and Development Finance

This chapter considers:

» the difficulty of cost-justifying training and development (T&D);
» matching individual training needs to performance imperatives; and
» the bridge between training and performance.

The words "Our people are our greatest asset" is probably one of the commonest phrases on the lips of chairmen and in company annual reports; but ask a few managers to name the easiest item in the management accounts to do without if times get hard and many will reply "Chop the training budget." This is particularly true of managers whose devotion to training and development is poor at the best of times, as in "Train a salesman, that's impossible. Salesmen are born not trained."

Hanging on to the T&D budget is hardest where senior managers do not see the item as connected to the performance of the organization in the same way as, for example, keeping up the research and development spend under all circumstances. Drop training and the short term changes little, making it easy to feel that you can catch up with it later; drop research and development and you know you are in trouble in the not-too-distant future.

The trouble is that an organization's whole cycle of planning and implementing the plan is just that – a cycle. If T&D are part of that cycle you cannot cut them and expect the rest of the wheel to go on as though nothing has happened (see Fig. 1.1).

And that is the organization's cycle. Now think about the individual. People know that if they go on learning they can perform better. They also know that their increased competencies allied to the improvement in performance makes them more marketable and more likely to become better paid and promoted; so they thirst for training and development. Senior management must supply this demand if they are to achieve higher goals in their plans, and keep the people that implement their plans well motivated. A professional team that is honest about its competencies and has its individual training needs aimed at meeting service or performance imperatives, is one that stays with an organization and consistently improves its performance.

And yet, cost-justification of the training and development budget never looks as easy as, for example, cost-justifying a computer system or spending money willy-nilly to restore competitiveness in a product or service.

This book will argue that training and development is as strategic to an organization's plan as anything else, and that if you fit training and development into the context of business performance, you actually make the short-term cost-justification easier. It should help individuals

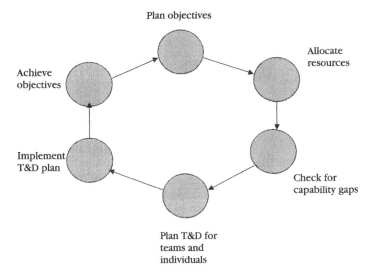

Fig. 1.1 The planning and training cycle.

trying to convince their managers of their need for, some would say right to, training, and functional managers defending attacks on the agreed training budget or proposing new expenditure in that area. It should also help training managers to show how their department links to the success and strategy of the organization and go for that bigger share of the expenditure cake.

It might even help chairmen to put their money where their mouth is and prove the real value their organization puts on its people. (That's if the next page on the annual report did not explain why they had, with regret, let 20% of their greatest asset go.)

Definition of Terms: What Does Managing Training and Development Finance Involve?

This chapter covers the definition of the following terms:

» performance deficits and interventions;
» T&D as a cost or an investment; and
» T&D as strategic to an organization.

PERFORMANCE DEFICITS AND INTERVENTIONS

Before considering the impact of training and development on correcting performance problems, let us not forget that training and development that are timed properly help to avoid such problems by preparing people for the tasks planned for them in the organization and team plan. It is as much part of the spectrum of people-management aimed at improving performance as the appraisal system or an organization's culture of leadership and openness.

But training and development also exist to correct problem areas where people are failing to perform to the standards expected of them (performance deficit); and to prepare people for tasks that they will be expected to do in the future, thus avoiding performance deficit. It is this linkage that forms the basis of managing the training and development (T&D) budget.

It is probably easiest to explain at the individual level. Before you can correct a problem you have to get a team member to agree in the first place that the problem exists. If they cannot see that their actions are having an adverse impact on meeting their objectives they will not commit to solving the problem. If you are able to show in detail how what they did affected the performance of them, their team or the organization, the team member can see why it is important to solve the problem. Asking questions to check that the team member does now agree that there is a problem, that they understand what it is and accept what the impact would be if the situation continues is part of basic appraisal technique. You should from this be able to calculate the financial repercussion of the problem, and you are on your way to cost-justifying the training and development solution.

Interventions, or T&D activities, address skills gaps agreed during appraisal or during planning. Most training happens on the job with the team leader as coach. Managers can use other methods, such as formal training courses, to accelerate the learning process. Ideally these should be thought through on an individual basis. What is this person's learning style? Do they learn quicker by doing things or having things demonstrated to them? Does reading books on the subject help them or would they do better using computer-based learning or a course? Success in training partly depends on the person's learning style. Much good research work has been done in this area, but we find the work of

Peter Honey and Alan Mumford in their book *The Manual of Learning Styles* (Honey, 1982) gets to the nub of the issue. Here is a summary of their work on learning styles, which they have identified in four groups.

» *Activist.* Activists involve themselves fully and without bias in new experiences. They enjoy the here-and-now and are happy to be dominated by immediate experiences. They are open-minded, not skeptical, and this tends to make them enthusiastic about anything new. They rush in where angels fear to tread.

» *Reflectors.* Reflectors like to stand back to ponder experiences and observe them from many different perspectives. They collect data, both first-hand and from others, and prefer to chew it over thoroughly before coming to any conclusions.

» *Theorists.* Theorists adapt and integrate observations into complex but logically sound theories. They think problems through in a vertical, step-by-step logical way. They assimilate disparate facts into coherent theories. They tend to be perfectionists who won't rest easy until things are tidy and fit into their rational scheme.

» *Pragmatists.* Pragmatists are keen on trying out ideas, theories, and techniques to see if they work in practice. They positively search out new ideas and take the first opportunity to experiment with applications. They are the sort of people who return from management courses brimming with new ideas that they want to try out in practice.

Thinking about an individual's learning style allows a manager to decide on what intervention is best before they plan the dates and organize the training. There are a wide range of T&D interventions:

» formal – conferences, training courses, qualifications;
» formal on-the-job – mentoring, coaching assignments, supervision, projects; and
» informal off-the-job – open learning, visits, self-study, briefing sessions, reflective practice.

The common factor in all of these is that they all cost money, both in terms of paying for the intervention, and in terms of time taken off the job.

IS TRAINING A COST OR AN INVESTMENT?

Many finance directors define costs as spending where no manager is responsible for proving the return or benefits that derive from the expenditure; the expenditure may or may not be necessary, but it is still a cost. An investment is a cost where a manager has proposed and taken responsibility for the return the organization should make on a given expenditure. If this is true, then we must not be surprised when some finance directors as well as some chief executives also regard the spending on training and development as a cost or an overhead.

A key message, therefore, about managing training and development finance is that managers must be prepared to justify the expenditure and get the agreement of finance that the training and development budget is indeed an investment. Nowadays most finance departments have moved from being obstructive towards training and development and become much more supportive of line managers. They try to use financial techniques to encourage managers to meet their objectives rather than a set of rules designed to stop initiatives and spending at all costs. They understand the concept of "strategic cost management" where investment is justified through its contribution to the organization's strategy rather than its day-to-day operation.

But they still have a duty to make sure that managers who are proposing spend in any area go through a proper process to demonstrate a good chance of making the return on investment required for spending an organization's money. So, it is useful to remember how obstructive FDs used to play the return-on-investment hurdle so that we can learn how to present a solid financial plan to back up the training and development plan itself. Think of how such a finance director approached the subject of benefits. They put them into three categories: reduction of cost, avoidance of costs, and improvements in control and performance.

In their risk analysis they paid most attention and gave most credence to proposals to reduce costs. Costs are actual and a reduction comes straight through as an improvement in profits or an extension of service in a non-profitmaking organization.

Avoidance of costs arises when a manager says that if we spend this money we will not have to spend further money in this new way. Once again an unenlightened finance director will give much less credence to this type of benefit on the grounds of "How can we be sure the costs would have arisen, or that they will not arise anyway?"

The third type links expenditure to improvement in control and performance, and is the least favorite of the three as far as our finance person is concerned. Indeed, skeptical finance people have been known to say that costs, in their experience, are absolutely real, while benefits are a sort of dream, argued at the time of making expenditure proposals but never tested or proven even after the event. Taking those lessons into account, we are better able to face modern finance departments with a strong linkage between performance monitoring and using T&D to change and improve performance for financial benefit.

In Chapter 6 (The State of the Art) and Chapter 7 (In Practice) we look further at cost justification and proving return on investment. It is not completely straightforward, but if you keep training finance in the context of the organization, it can be done.

TRAINING AND DEVELOPMENT IS STRATEGIC

But the starting point of managing training and development finance is to look at it strategically, as demonstrably most successful organizations do. The strategy of any organization depends at some point on its people. The competition to recruit the right people and retain them is intense even when, as at the time of writing, the economy is not growing hugely and some industries, telecommunications for example, are letting a lot of people go. It is easier to retain the people you are not too worried about than the ones who seem vital to the organization. Indeed, taking training away from people because of budget cuts is counterproductive if it weakens your ability to hold on to such important people. Add to this the fact that neither organizations nor their people nowadays give much credence to the "job for life" and you realize the huge necessity of meeting people's aspirations for training.

Increasingly, employees have high expectations of their employer – the stakes are high in the "staff retention" game. There's always someone else who will offer more promotional opportunities and more development. This pushes some managers into offering training with little thought to the appropriateness, return and so on. They are driven by push from their people, and are unlikely to be considered too kindly by a good financial controller. Conversely, some managers in organizations where short-term cost management is a core driver, feel truly constrained in providing training and development opportunities where the return on investment or the product-purchased fees can be somewhat nebulous.

Managing T&D finance is about applying strategic importance to T&D such that it is rigorously defined and justified, rather than just treating it as a "free good" or perk. Training is no more than a "free good" when there is no discernible payback from the individual going on training interventions and where the training is not set in the context of performance improvement goals. It is part of the *business* to define skills, knowledge and behavior deficits that need to be brought into balance to achieve its objectives, or for the organization with major growth imperatives to turn them into surpluses.

Too often, spend on people in organizations is not treated in the same way as the purchase of IT equipment even though the financial consequences are far deeper and longer-term. When one of the authors was an HR professional it was a real frustration for her that CEOs and line managers resisted understanding the true cost of their HR processes – recruitment, performance management as well as training. It never ceased to amaze her that companies would be quite happy to centralize PC purchasing (having many authorizing levels for a spend of £1000) but would delegate, with no form of monitoring, the acquisition and maintenance of its human resource (an expenditure of some £24,000 before on-costs on average in the UK today).

It could be much harder to challenge a line manager on decisions about spend on their people than tiny capital-spend decisions – an example of a failure to really value "this organization's greatest asset." There is a fantasy in an organization that is weak on people, or among weak managers, that being nice and supportive, kind and cuddly in people resource management, and being driven by individuals' requests for development with little or no scrutiny, looks like good people management and valuing people – but it is actually the opposite.

We should look for control and processes that empower managers and teams to see their training and development in the same way as maintaining basic equipment for the job – in fact there is a real difference in that you can get a much better return from, as it were, maintaining your people than from any IT or medical equipment.

In the end, tackling T&D as strategic allows organizations to understand what they are spending in this area and to direct it better. This makes the organization challenge its team leaders to develop an annual T&D financial planning cycle in the same way that they will look at pay costs and non-pay costs. After all, many organizations are known to spend, say, £800 per head on T&D and some would say that much of that shows no proven return.

In their book *Competing in the Third Wave* (Harvard Business School Press, 1997), Jeremy Hope and Tony Hope quote an article in *Training* magazine that states that:

> "American corporations spend more than $50 billion on formal training and as much as half of this gargantuan expenditure is being utterly wasted – squandered on training that's unnecessary, training that's aimed at non-training problems, and training that's doomed by its poor design. Corporate training is failing to deal with the individual needs of its students. Classroom training delivers too much or too little, too early or too late, and is too expensive."

Even if this assessment is only half right, it does demonstrate that a strategic approach to training, rather than an approach with no overview or corporate interest in individual managers, is essential if a company is to have a chance of making training pay.

KEY LEARNING POINTS

- It is perilous to mess around with training spend. Freezing it can cost the organization more in dropping morale than it saves in costs.
- A hierarchy of training strategies connected to the hierarchy of business plans and objectives leads to stabilization of T&D finance and recognition that it is in fact an investment. More of this follows in Chapter 3 on the evolution of T&D.

» Investing in team-working training and development is a given in any successful organization nowadays.
» The T&D plan derives from the appraisal and development plan processes in the organization.

Evolution of Managing Training and Development Finance

This chapter looks at the evolution, over the years, of current thinking about managing training and development finance in terms of:

» the time-line of evolution in T&D finance;
» a checklist of costs and benefits; and
» connecting training to the job.

INTRODUCTION

In a world where team leaders do not focus on their primary task effectively, training is likely to be opportunistic – we do what is easy to put in place in response to an individual or a particular situation. Some people still do not believe that they are responsible for the overall competencies of their people nor feel able to make a training proposal robust by showing how it supports the improvement in completing a particular task. And yet despite this reality, over time, training and development (T&D) has become strategic to organizations. How have we got to this situation, and how do we need to evolve further, to meet modern-day requirements?

THE TIME-LINE OF EVOLUTION

Samuel Whitbread was born in 1720 and began his apprenticeship as a brewer in 1736. Only six years later he was in a position to found his first brewery. From the few details of his apprenticeship we have, we can suppose that he worked hard for very little money, and from his subsequent success assume that he learnt fast and well. He had no day-release to the local further education institute but learnt all he needed as he went about the job of brewing.

According to their Website, the Company of Cutlers was formed in 1624 in Sheffield. A key function of the company was to bind and free apprentices. The apprentice and his master each had duties and obligations. As well as teaching the apprentice the skills of his trade, the master agreed to provide the apprentice with all his needs – food, clothing and lodging. He also agreed to pay him one shilling per year (this is at the beginning of the eighteenth century). In return, the apprentice agreed to live like a saint, not get married, not frequent taverns or alehouses, and not play any unlawful games. He agreed to live in his master's house and not be absent from work for more than 14 days per year without good cause. An apprenticeship lasted for seven years.

By the nineteenth century there were apprenticeships available with full on-the-job training; but the trainees and families expected to pay for the privilege of being trained and the people doing the training did not expect to pay the trainees during their apprenticeship period. The professions too, lawyers and doctors for example, expected their apprentices to pay their own way, and in fact there are still some vestiges of this approach in the UK.

After World War II such a scheme of patronage gradually lost support. By the 60s and 70s, a period of high employment, young people were reluctant to take up apprenticeships where they worked for very low wages for five years before becoming "qualified" to do the job for a proper return. Employers also, in an increasingly competitive environment, were reluctant to invest in young people. However, there were millions who left school with few, if any, qualifications, entering a world of work that would offer little or no training, no opportunity to develop themselves and no recognition for any competencies they did develop.

The traditional apprenticeship system started to collapse. Young people failed to find training, skill shortages arose, and businesses, the national economy, and the UK's competitiveness suffered. It was clear that something had to be done.

In 1981 the government stepped in, setting up the Manpower Services Commission (a predecessor of the DfEE). Two of the main themes of the Commission were about occupational standards and young people. From that point, the UK started to develop occupational standards within each industry, each industry taking responsibility for itself.

Also in the early 1980s, unemployment amongst young people was becoming a serious issue. The existing program for youth training, funded by the government, had been expanded but still could only offer uncertificated training that left employers unsure of what these potential employees could actually do, and the trainees often unable to convince employers about the depth, range, and quality of what they had learnt.

In 1986 the government established the National Council for Vocational Qualifications (NCVQ) – to set up a comprehensive framework of vocational qualifications covering all occupations and industries. The first award – at level two – was made in 1988.

Employers were central – they needed to be persuaded to agree common standards for all occupations within their industries. Also vital were the organizations that actually provided training and awarded certificates. In the mid-1980s, training providers and awarding bodies could set their own agendas with no regard for the needs of industry, the economy, or the national skill needs. Two agendas were set – the training of skilled workpeople was a combination of classroom and on-the-job training, and the government became increasingly involved in the training of the workforce.

All through the twentieth century, people under training worked for lower salaries than the trained employee. But technology, society change, and increased employment led to employee expectations of training and development expenditure eventually being seen as a right.

Changes in society included more centralized government economic control, and ensured that T&D finance moved into the political arena. Economists advised the government that planning and controlling the economy included taking action to make sure the right amount of the right training was in place to keep the workforce competitive. This has caused the state funding of training to grow over the years.

Also through the latter part of the twentieth century was the growth in training for skills such as sales and marketing – for example, the first sales school was set up for NCR in America in the early 1900s. And, of course, there emerged the burgeoning business of management training.

During the 80s and 90s Fiona, one of the authors, was involved in implementing policies that tried to establish mutual responsibility between employee and employer for high training costs. This included the trade-off of the organization funding further degrees, for example, in return for handcuffing people to periods of time with the employer post-qualification. If they left too soon they had to pay something back. This promoted a large focus on training and development as a specialist function within organizations that left the planning and direction of T&D to a specialist in, for example, the HR function.

Most senior HR and T&D specialists feel that in this century these sorts of arrangements are out-of-date. We have evolved to a position where training expenditure has to be part of the business planning process and organization culture rather than being individually based and reactive.

Take the example of technology. The many adults at work now in their 30s and 40s, born before 1970, did not get any training or practice with computers during their education. To those at work now who were born after 1970, computers are like pen and paper.

Computer literacy is therefore the equivalent to the literacy requirements recognized by governments who brought in education for all in the nineteenth century. Organizations have obviously built this training requirement automatically into their financial plans nowadays, not daring to think of the cost of not doing so. But in this example, not everyone in the organization needs to be as computer-literate as the engineers and specialists who depend on using computers innovatively to succeed in their jobs.

So, the importance of team leaders in their role in T&D finance has grown. What was previously a centralized function is now increasingly devolved as a core supervisory role. Organizations now require team leaders to develop their business planning, budget setting and managing skills first, and then start to incorporate the right amount of T&D into their budgets. A good team leader will find ways to do this without being prompted. There was no expectation 20 years ago that a team leader would do this and business processes and systems didn't support this level of delegation.

COST-BENEFIT ANALYSIS

In the end, though, team leaders and managers have to make pragmatic business cases to support their requests for T&D budgets. And time has evolved this checklist of benefits that are available for training, most of which can be calculated financially.

Checklist of benefits

1 Training helps employees to learn their jobs quickly and effectively, thus minimizing learning costs and getting people to make a positive contribution earlier.
2 Existing staff can be helped by training to improve their work performance and to keep up-to-date in their specialist fields.
3 A greater volume of work can be expected from trained staff, partly because they work more rapidly and partly because they make fewer mistakes.
4 A reduction in work-errors benefits an organization in two other ways – management can spend more time on planning and development activities instead of correcting mistakes, and costs of correcting errors are eliminated.

5 Staff satisfaction is increased, which helps staff retention.

6 Retained staff need retraining to replace obsolete skills.

7 Training in safe working practices reduces accidents, resulting in social and financial benefits to employers, employees, and society.

8 A reputation for training helps an organization attract good job applicants.

9 Employees are less likely to become frustrated and leave if training and development opportunities are available for furthering their careers with their current employer.

10 An organization needs a flexible workforce to operate efficiently when people are absent through sickness or holiday. Training increases employees' versatility by extending their range of expertise to include related jobs.

11 The general morale of an organization is enhanced by effective organization development (OD) and individual employee training interventions. Taken together, these approaches can improve an organization's ability to accept and implement change, to become more proactive, and so be able to take greater advantage of new opportunities.

Checklist of learning costs

1 Payments made to employees when first learning their jobs or when undergoing refresher training.

2 Costs of materials wasted, sales lost, or incorrect decisions made as learners acquire competence.

3 Cost of reduced output caused by the detrimental effect learners can have on those with whom they are working.

4 Costs resulting from employees leaving the organization because they find the work too difficult.

5 Costs attributed to accidents caused by inexperience or ignorance.

Checklist of training costs

1 Capital and running costs of a training center.

2 People costs – managers' pay as they coach, trainers' fees, expenses for attending courses.

3 Equipment costs.

4 Materials costs.

The source of much of the above is *Training Interventions* (John Kenney & Margaret Reid, Institute of Personnel Management, 1986).

CONNECTING TRAINING TO THE JOB

So the evolution of managing the training and development function has, some would say, gone full circle. The days when craftsmen taught their apprentices by demonstration, and encouragement to learn by doing the job, gradually moved to a period when classroom training became a distinguishing factor that employees took into account when choosing for whom to work. Mirrored with this rise in formal training interventions was the rise in management and training consultants, charging very high daily rates and, in many cases, being effective in the classroom but having less effect on the performance of the organization.

We now know that the T&D budget needs to be a blend of formal interventions and learning at the point of doing the job. That way the training has to fit the operation on the ground, using the same processes in the classroom as are used in the field. The connection of objective to process and process to training has never been closer.

On the development side, a successful organization knows that its strategic plan can never stand still. Gone are the days when the board could wait for its annual weekend off-site to think about the way ahead. A move by a competitor can enforce a change in strategy almost overnight in some industries. In that environment, team strategies and their attendant T&D strategies have to be agile enough to keep up.

A very good example of using training in a major reformation of an organization is found in a company like GE. They used the Six Sigma tools and processes to improve their performance to their customers to an extent where the number of times they failed to meet customer requirements dropped to a theoretical 3.4 defects in every million opportunities. (That is the statistical aspiration behind the Six Sigma culture). In so doing, their chief executive Jack Welch was able to write in the annual report that in just three years Six Sigma had saved the company more than $2bn, against costs calculated at $1bn, a healthy rate of return for a massive spend. Much of that spend was on intensive training at senior- and middle-management level and corporate-wide training at other levels. The training enables the teams to find ways to improve the processes, to reduce defects in customer satisfaction, and to improve profits; and then the training helps the owners of the new processes to implement them, and achieve the expected financial results.

In Chapter 4 (The E-Dimension) we will talk about technology offering more and more opportunities for cost-effective learning at the point of doing. Who knows, if we get it right perhaps we can produce trainees who, like Sam Whitbread, can go from cleaning barrels to owning their own brewery in six short years.

KEY LEARNING POINTS

» The funding of training has moved over time from the employee to the employer, and now consists of a balance between central and local government and employers.

» From the textbooks we can derive a checklist of possible costs and benefits that we can transfer into the business case for investing in training by attaching specific values to the benefits, and correctly estimating *all* the costs.

» Learning at the point of doing is a growing technique in training interventions due to its obvious payback: you can see the job done better there and then, and because technology allows this to be controlled and built into everyday business processes.

» There is ample room for improvement in managing T&D finance, since much of the money in current budgets cannot be connected to the employee adding value to the customer's requirement for products and services.

The E-Dimension

This chapter looks at the considerable opportunities that the e-dimension offers to team leaders and their people in terms of:

» the e-dimension as a method of improving the cost-effectiveness of training; and
» the Internet as a source of information.

LEARNING AT THE POINT OF DOING THE JOB

Face-to-face classroom training is probably the most effective way of assisting people to learn new skills and change their behavior in everyday business life. It is certainly the most expensive. There is the cost of the trainers, internal or external to the organization, the cost of the venue, possibly overnight stays for the delegates, and so on. And that is before you add the biggest cost of the lot – the cost of having members of staff not available for work while they are on training.

Various attempts have been made to use the e-dimension to lower the price of training and improve its effectiveness, with varying degrees of success. E-learning, with its emphasis on making information available on a screen, has a role to play in this, but we want to look in this chapter at one of the most effective ways of exploiting the Web for training budget purposes – the combination of classroom training, practical business processes, and online coaching. For want of a better term, this "blended solution" to the training problem has potentially a most dramatic impact on the effective use of training and development finance.

Think of it this way. Suppose you have to train a bunch of young people to carry out interviews on behalf of a building society or bank, where the objective is to sell mortgage finance. Actually, it is the easiest thing in the world to sell mortgage finance, since the only people who come to the interview are those who have found a house they want to buy and lack the funds to make the purchase without borrowing. Even the most butter-fingered salesman is going to succeed in that situation. In fact, the job of training mortgage interviewers is much more about cross-selling house and other insurances offering a high profit margin on an annual basis, than about selling the mortgage, which is, in fact, very low-margin business. The skills required include customer awareness, asking open questions, and listening and reacting to the answers – a classic area for classroom training, with its ability to use, for example, role-play practice for each delegate.

Such training is done very effectively because the business process involved, the filling-in of the mortgage form, is already part of everyday life in the branch. The trainers are not introducing any new process, and when the delegates go back to the field there is no option to ignore the process taught in the classroom. So the trainers can concentrate on helping delegates to bring up the subject of insurance early in the interview, ask about dependants, smile, use the name of the interviewee regularly, and so on.

How different this is in a less process-oriented environment, such as training salespeople on handling complex sales campaigns. Here the trainer is faced not only with teaching the selling skills involved in selling solutions rather than products, but also with persuading the delegates to operate new campaign-planning processes that are not necessarily in everyday use back in the field. Not only that, but the processes may be completely new to the sales manager to whom the salesperson reports in the real world. If the manager does not reinforce the use of the process back in the field, it will almost certainly wither and die, substantially reducing the effectiveness of the training intervention.

Figure 4.1 shows this decline as the line leading from the training intervention to A: ignore and forget. If, however, you adopt the ideas of the building society and use training to concentrate on skills and understanding by using processes that are already implemented in the field, you can change this decline to the line B and sustain the training when the trainees return to the field. If, in addition to the business process involved, you make further knowledge available through a combination of online coaching, the use of forums, and giving access to

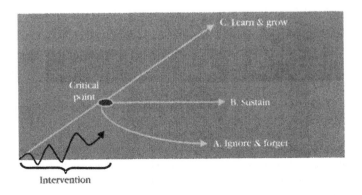

Fig. 4.1 Connecting business processes with training.

the work of people who have used the process before, the effectiveness of the expensive classroom part of the training is enhanced by the continuation of learning back on the job – line C: learn and grow. This is what the e-dimension in training and development offers to forward-looking organizations.

Let us take a detailed example of how the electronic back-up enhances the cost-effectiveness of training. We will take an interpersonal skills issue – the writing of executive summaries of business proposals, in this case for salespeople, but a skill that any manager needs to be able to do well.

Here are some facts surrounding the real situation in many organizations in developing complex sales campaigns.

» Sales managers often get sight of a complex sales proposal just before or just after submission to the customer. This means that it is too late for them to add value to the document even if they have information gained from other campaigns that would have improved the proposal considerably.

» Salespeople learn remarkably little from each other in terms of expressing vital parts of a sales proposal, such as the customer's basis of decision or the selling company's winning strategy. They may copy huge chunks of product description from marketing brochures, but are on their own when it comes to the vital bit of a sales proposal – the *executive summary*.

» Many sales proposals are completed at two o'clock in the morning when there are no other salespeople to consult.

» The executive summary is often left until the last thing. This means that the focus of the sales campaign is not available to the selling team while they are dealing with the customer.

The e-dimension in T&D solves all of these problems by using a simple electronic tool – the *executive summary data sheet*.

Imagine if each salesperson was taught in the classroom how to use this executive summary template to summarize the position in each sales campaign and everyone who needed it had access to it on the company's intranet. Salespeople, even at two o'clock in the morning, would be able to look at a number of previous executive summaries to find a *mot juste* to describe a particular benefit, or a neat piece

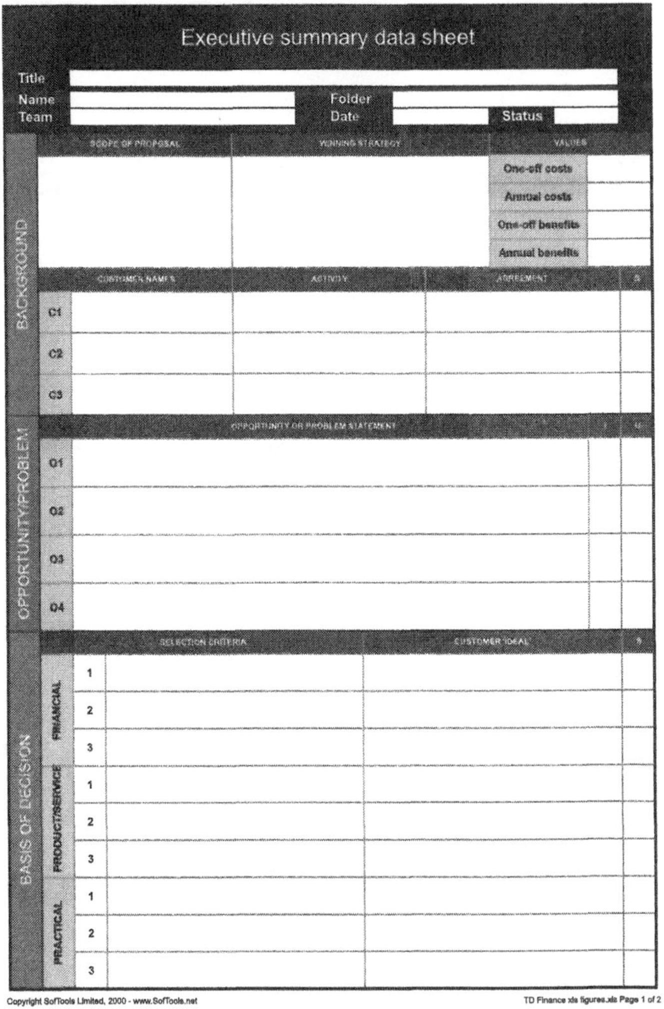
Executive summary data sheet

Title

Name | Folder

Team | Date | Status

BACKGROUND

SCOPE OF PROPOSAL | WINNING STRATEGY | VALUES

One-off costs

Annual costs

One-off benefits

Annual benefits

CUSTOMER NAMES | ACTIVITY | AGREEMENT | S

C1

C2

C3

OPPORTUNITY/PROBLEM

OPPORTUNITY OR PROBLEM STATEMENT | I | U

O1

O2

O3

O4

BASIS OF DECISION

SELECTION CRITERIA | CUSTOMER 'IDEAL' | %

FINANCIAL 1, 2, 3

PRODUCT/SERVICE 1, 2, 3

PRACTICAL 1, 2, 3

Copyright SofTools Limited, 2000 - www.SofTools.net

TD Finance xls figures.xls Page 1 of 2

Fig. 4.2 Executive summary data sheet.

PROPOSAL		PROPOSAL ELEMENTS								ONE-OFF		ANNUAL	
	Product	TVdesserT range											
	Service	Rapid reaction delivery service											
	After sales service	Re-promotion for selected stores											
							TOTAL COSTS						

BENEFITS			BUSINESS BENEFIT							ONE-OFF		ANNUAL	
	TANGIBLE	Increased revenues											
		Reduced costs											
		Avoid costs											
							TOTAL BENEFITS						
	INTANGIBLE	Management control											
		Customer satisfaction											
		Competitive edge											

IMPLEMENTATION PLAN		TASKS		START	END	Q1	Q2	Q3	Q4	Q5	Q6	Q7	Q8
	T1												
	T2												
	T3												
	T4												
	T5												
	T6												
	T7												
	T8												
	T9												
	T10												

NEXT STEPS		RECOMMENDED ACTIONS		OWNER	DATE
	A1				
	A2				
	A3				

Fig. 4.2 *(continued)*

of purple prose that a salesperson had used in previous proposals to describe why a customer should buy from this particular organization.

Think of the control the sales managers would have if they were able to go online and look at the current state of every sales campaign, or perhaps every sales campaign with a value greater than $50,000. Figure 4.2 shows what such an electronic tool looks like, and is followed by an explanation.

EXECUTIVE SUMMARY DATA SHEET

Salespeople begin to prepare the data sheet the moment they have identified a sales campaign and agreed to carry it out. The sooner in the campaign they can answer the questions it raises, the clearer will be their strategy. This gives them selling focus and allows them to brief all the managers, product experts and commercial people involved in the campaign so that they act consistently and support the salesperson's overall approach.

In the classroom they are taught that it is unlikely for any campaign that they will have a full and satisfactory answer to every question, but the nearer they can get to that, the more likely they are to win the campaign, and equally importantly, the easier it will be to produce an interesting and compelling executive summary for their senior customer managers. Back in the field the trainer will continue to monitor the training delegates they met in the classroom until, say, they have completed two executive summary data sheets.

One of the many benefits of this approach is that it does not depend on all the delegates completing the exercise in the classroom. This cuts down the amount of time spent with half the class waiting for the other half to finish off. From experience, this approach also cuts down the amount of time needed in the classroom from two days to one – a huge saving of costs of training and the opportunity cost of people being back on the job for the second day.

This is, then, an internal document that contains everything salespeople need to produce the executive summary for delivery to senior customer managers towards the end of a sales campaign.

- *Background* – this makes them trust you as a salesperson to have done the appropriate work and spoken to the appropriate people.
- *Scope* – this explains the boundaries of the proposal.
- *Winning strategy* – this is a short statement of why the selling organization will win this particular piece of business.
- *Costs and benefits* – here the salesperson enters the costs of the proposal together with the financial benefits they have agreed with the customer during the campaign.
- *Customer name, activity, and agreement* – here they state the names of the customer's people you have worked with in preparing the proposal. The status box should be marked red, amber, or green to show how far you have got during the campaign to get these important agreements.
- *The customer problem or opportunity* – after reading this, managers will understand in more detail what the proposal is for, and will have a snapshot of the business benefit that will occur.
- *Problem or opportunity statement* – explain in their terms what problem you are solving with this proposal or what is their opportunity that you are helping them to exploit.
- *Impact* – in the summary they will comment on what they have been told of the impact of the problem or the significance of the opportunity.
- *Urgency* – this records how urgent it is to solve the problem or how significant it is from a competitive point of view for the customer to exploit the opportunity.
- *Value* – for each statement, the salesperson gives an indication of the value of the opportunity or perhaps the cost of the problem.
- *The basis of decision* – salespeople need to show them that they can see the decision to go ahead from the customer's point of view. In effect, they are telling them what to look for in our submission.
- *Selection criteria* – this is a statement of each decision criterion, along with what the customer ideally wants in this regard.

> *Status* – again red, amber, or green to show how much work they need to do to get nearer to the ideal.
> *The supplier proposal* – this is a simple statement in customer terms of what the supplier is proposing they buy and do. It tries to avoid jargon.
> *Proposal elements* – this is kept simple and high-level.
> *Capital* – the capital costs of each element.
> *Revenue* – the revenue or ongoing costs, probably on an annual basis.
> *Benefits* – this gives the customer a clear idea of the business benefits and who, in their organization, is taking responsibility for achieving them.
> *Business benefit* – a statement of the customer business benefit.
> *Implementation plan* – the supplying team and the customer, either separately or together, will probably have a project plan by the time it comes to writing the executive summary.
> *Recommended actions* – the objective of the executive summary is to encourage and persuade someone to do something. This section records what those short-term actions are.

Integrated Performance Support Systems

The e-dimension needs a software platform as a basis for supporting training and development. It has the following elements.

1 *Processes and tools* – structured templates reflecting organization-specific processes, from business planning to risk management, to calculating return on investment, as examples.
2 *Online coach* – online self-paced learning environment, including the content part – perhaps many e-reports and books offering "learning-at-the-point-of-doing."
3 *Experts* – access to the ideas and insights of internal and external experts.
4 *Forum* – open discussion of ideas relating to projects, teams, or competency areas.
5 *Knowledge base* – visibility and retrieval of real project or case files, both current and historic.

6 *Portfolio status* – production of key management reports covering individual and team performance.

Such a platform is available through SofTools Ltd. You can reach them on www.SofTools.net

THE INTERNET AS A SOURCE OF INFORMATION

Most people can do their jobs better at a very reasonable cost if they are aware of the resources available to them from the Internet. This part of the T&D budget is hard to describe without taking the example of an actual industry. The National Health Service in the UK organizes access to and training about their intranets and extranets for both managers and clinicians. At NHS Trust level, the main management divisions in the NHS, and at national level, much work has been done. Here are some examples of how the NHS goes about it.

The Internet as a research and development tool

Recognizing the Internet and access to it as a basic tool of many jobs, the NHS has an "Access to the Internet" project for clinicians. This aims to ensure that sufficient equipment is available to enable clinicians to check evidence for particular treatments, or protocols, access research to develop knowledge, and so on. To support the use of this resource, and in the research area generally, clinicians should have access to both technical and research training and development – such as Critical Appraisal Training – enabling people to train in techniques to sift information and determine usefulness.

Getting on Board the Net

Getting on Board the Net (Robert Kley, Peter Davies, Elizabeth Graham, NHS Confederation, 2002) is a booklet designed to help non-clinical people to access and use the Internet for interactive learning, information resources, and potential T&D resources. In addition to this, NHS Trust intranets are examples of knowledge libraries for people to access as part of their learning. Outside of the Trusts themselves there are nationally available extranets. For example, NHSnet is an information and knowledge database for people to access at work or at home, rather than attend courses or buy books.

Website www.doh.gov.uk is the official government site for the NHS in England, primarily of use to health and social care professionals as well as academics. It is an important source for people to study policy papers. In over 20 useful parts of the Department of Health site there are sources of information, knowledge, and best practice. Good use of these resources leads to people not having to attend some courses and seminars as their knowledge and familiarity with the Internet develops.

NHS best practice on the Internet

(The source for this material is *Getting on Board the Net, above*)

» *Bradford Health and Social Care Community* – the Website promotes, supports, and encourages learning and continuous professional development for everyone working in health and social care in Bradford. It provides a one-stop-shop to keep them informed of what's happening in education and training in the district and beyond, including a calendar of events and courses, as well as a resource bank of templates, protocols, and other examples of good practice.

Link: www.learnonline.nhs.uk

» *Medical database online* – produced by the US National Library of Medicine, *Medline* is the world's leading database. Dates from 1966 (printed *Index Medicus* dates from 1879). Contains 11 million bibliographic references and abstracts drawn from more than 4300 biomedical journals. This database is mainly used to identify published research on a specific topic.

Link: www.ncbi.nlm.nih.gov/entrez/query.fcgi

KEY LEARNING POINT

One of the greatest problems facing managers is to get people to help each other by sharing experience. If they build an electronic process into the normal business day and insist on its being

The Global Dimension

This chapter looks at the threat posed by global stakeholders in managing training and development finance planning in terms of:

» the centralize/decentralize argument in T&D planning;
» the cultural dilemma at different levels of training spend; and
» maintaining a global T&D plan.

THE CENTRALIZE/DECENTRALIZE ARGUMENT IN PLANNING AND BUDGETING

In a global environment the development of the international manager in all functions, including HR, has become a strategic activity. In developing truly international managers, organizations are simultaneously fostering their own process of becoming international in outlook and practice. Central to this process is awareness of, and respect for cultural diversity.

The successful international manager has to reconcile a number of key dilemmas common to all cultures. How do you expand the ethos and culture that has made the organization successful, while recognizing that compromises have to be made to deal with local traditions and rules? Failure to reconcile these dilemmas will lead to the failure of an organization's international aspirations and strategies.

Management in a global environment is increasingly affected by cultural differences. The way it is deployed in a multicultural environment is, and needs to be, dependent on the broader strategy. It also reflects how truly international an organization is and, it is to be hoped, the level of internationalization of the corporation.

Basic in understanding other cultures is the awareness that culture is a series of rules and methods that a society has evolved to deal with the recurring problems it faces. They have become so basic that, like breathing, we no longer think about how we approach or resolve them. Every country and every organization faces dilemmas in relationships with people; dilemmas in relationship to time; and dilemmas in relations between people and the natural environment. Culture is the way in which people resolve dilemmas emerging from universal problems.

While nations differ markedly in how they approach these dilemmas, they do not differ in needing to make some kind of response. The successful international manager is in a position to reconcile dilemmas more effectively by building a strategy that can be implemented consistently throughout the organization.

In budgeting terms, consideration of the global dimension starts from understanding the reality of cultural differences and moves towards cost comparisons between central budgets and local ones.

THE CULTURAL DILEMMA AT DIFFERENT LEVELS OF TRAINING SPEND

This cultural dilemma is clearly seen in the training and development area, given the model explored in more detail in Chapter 6 (The State of the Art):

» Level 1: Organizational training and development sponsored at the CEO level.
» Level 2: Resources managed at the organizational level by the HR function.
» Level 3: Departmental training and development organized by the team leader.
» Level 4: Individuals' responsibilities for their own needs.

Perhaps the biggest threat is in the Level 1 area. If an organization is developing a cultural change in its domestic operation, such as core process design or Six Sigma, it must be careful to obey the rules of respecting national diversity most carefully.

This needs to go beyond simple awareness of cultural differences. The roll-out of such programs needs to respect these differences and take advantage of diversity through reconciling cross-cultural dilemmas. The international manager has a role in reconciling cultural dilemmas.

Like any major change program, the spreading out of a training and development initiative on a worldwide basis stands or falls by the active co-operation of local people. The rule of thumb in managing change is that it takes 20% of the people who need to change how they work to be active supporters or "agents of change." Once you have such a group on board, you can start the work on the other 80% with a good chance of success.

Managers should never underestimate the depth of cultural diversity. Here are two simple examples learned from the experience of taking a similar training program into different cultures.

A UK-based trainer has successfully implemented a major change program in an American company. HR in the UK invites the senior managers of the USA enterprise to attend a shortened version of the course to see if it could be a shortcut to handling a similar change in the USA. They are enthusiastic about this and invite the same external training organization to implement the program in the States.

Now, non-international people from the UK tend in the first place to treat Americans as basically English people with a funny accent – they wise-up pretty soon.

This next example is something of a generalization, but it stands the test of experience. Take a simple thing like feedback to the first training event itself. In the UK a delegate on a training course will challenge the trainer in the classroom quite assertively until they become convinced of the merit of the argument being made. If by the end of the program they are still undecided whether to accept the change of behavior being proposed, they will continue to challenge and question. Americans join a class and will use phrases in their introduction like "My name is X and I am happy to be here," an opening that most UK people would find unacceptable until the event proves itself.

So the trainer in the UK gets continuous feedback and reasonably easily can measure where they are and how well they are achieving the objectives set for the event.

In the USA feedback during the program is much less helpful, and many trainers working in that environment can be taken by complete surprise when they get feedback tick-sheets at the end of the event, showing resistance to the changes promoted in the program. USA people don't talk about it in the classroom, but they can hit pretty hard on the feedback forms. In the UK, people can give trainers a hard time during the event, but give much more positive feedback on the official forms.

These are just facts, but they need to be built into the planning of any training roll-out and pretty much make the case for getting local people trained to implement programs as quickly as possible, no matter how unique the processes or ideas that the person from overseas brings in.

Let's go now to Hong Kong and consider an Australian sales-training consultancy taking a similar roll-out program, successfully implemented in their country, there. Being a sales training course, the Australian version had a hugely competitive element, with four teams going through a simulated sales campaign, ending with a final presentation to the board. The people on the course wanted to know who had won at the end. Trying the same technique in Hong Kong failed to promote the competitive spirit. The trainers at the final presentation were taken aback to be given the same presentation by the four teams, who had got together the previous evening to make sure that no one lost face on the final day by not being in the winning team. This does not mean that the event failed to meet the training objectives; it just proves that the cultural difference required a different approach to this part of the course.

Simple examples, but illustrative of the care needed when planning international initiatives at the top level sponsored by top management.

Level 2 training, supported by the central HR function, offers similar dilemmas to the Level 1 spend, but tends to be more in terms of maintaining continuity amongst local plans than about the imposition of change and other types of program throughout the organization. It is, however, an important role. Gone are the days when companies could afford the luxury of reinventing the wheel in different parts of the globe by having no centralized scrutiny of training and development spend. Central HR needs to lay down the rules clearly, spelling out where different programs are being examined and preventing two geographic locations finding two dissimilar solutions to the kind of programs involved in Level 2. For their part, local HR and local functional managers must include central HR in the stakeholders to be advised and listened to when they are planning new initiatives.

The diversity problems diminish at Levels 3 and 4 training spend, with the locations making their own decisions about training and development and about the allocation of budgets.

It is worth remembering at this point the true costs of training. The main cost of a training event is the cost of travel for the delegates, their accommodation and other items, and, of course, the huge opportunity cost present because people are being taken off the job for a period of unproductive time while they are in a classroom. The impact of this is that the travel and accommodation costs of international trainers are much less of an issue than it seems at first. So, the decision to fly an expert in, or find a local solution, can be based on the real benefits picture rather than the simple question of air-fares.

MAINTAINING A GLOBAL PLAN

E-learning is becoming an essential component of an organization's total development program because of its cost-effective nature and its reinforcement of ideas on-the-job. Organizations recognize that their real competitive advantage lies in the combined knowledge and experience of their functional managers and their HR teams. Process skills and knowledge are now part of what is referred to as an organization's "intellectual capital." *Knowledge management* is the term used to reflect getting the right information to the right people at the right time, and is quickly becoming a core competence of modern HR management.

This is true from the information gathered about Internet and other resources being available to all geographic locations involved in the plan, to simple things like a forum that all HR people regularly access to keep up to date with what different geographies are doing. But, the key to linking the activities of the whole function on a global basis is the development of and access to the global plans.

KEY LEARNING POINTS

» Senior management trying to organize a global initiative must take into account local geography and managers' views as to how the different cultural values involved will accept the initiative.

» It is generally better to use local training resources than fly in visitors from different cultures.

» In organizational training and process-change initiatives, overseas geographies need to be involved in the planning process.

The State of the Art

This chapter looks at the elements involved in creating:

» a model for planning and allocating resources to T&D;
» the link between this model and the cost-justification of T&D; and
» an electronic template for assessing return on investment.

A MODERN-DAY MODEL FOR MANAGING T&D FINANCE

The model Fiona works with nowadays has four levels, with financial plans applied at each level, all of which are shaped and determined by the organization's key strategic objectives.

Level 1. Organization level and the CEO's responsibility

The CEO directs and financially supports interventions from a central budget for the following purposes.

» Organizational change (in the jargon, "Organization Development") interventions, where large groups of key leaders and individuals come together to develop a common sense of purpose and a picture for the future. These interventions are in various forms with a number of different types of facilitation or process.
» Team-working: special attention is applied to the functioning of the top team as a team and as leaders. The top team drives the leadership style, the open culture and the emphasis on teamwork for the organization, and therefore needs special investment. It should also act as a model for team-working within the organization as a whole.
» Support for team leaders across the organization to access specialist resources, and funds to develop their teams' performance and effective functioning.
» Management/supervisor leadership development. Definition and direction of programs specifically designed to meet CEOs' expectations of team leaders as people-managers.

Level 2. Resource managed at the organization level, usually the HR and Quality Improvement functions' responsibility

A resource for technical knowledge and skills to deliver the organization's services/products; also to ensure effective T&D across the organization. This spend pays for the following.

» A specialist development function to ensure promotion of and access to technical development, as well as effective resource allocation and management.
» Mandatory training to meet statutory requirements and organizational requirements, e.g. health and safety, people management, and meetings management.
» An organizational model for appraisal and personal development plans (PDPs).
» Training programs in effective appraisal and PDPs.
» Template process for departmental T&D plans.
» Core generic skills and process programs.

Level 3. At departmental level, the team leader's responsibilities

» Development plan for the team, based on what's available and required in Levels 1 and 2.
» Linking that plan to individual performance requirements and career aspirations discovered in the appraisal and PDP process.
» Talking to their people, team leaders or individuals, continuously, about what they expect them to be doing for themselves, using as a model the responsibilities of the individual listed below.

Level 4. Each individual's responsibilities

» Their own personal development and personal leadership; understanding this in the context of both their current role and their future aspirations.
» Agreeing a cost-and-obligation equation, where their contribution to the organization reflects the amount of individual, or additional, expenditure the organization puts into their development. For example, Fiona's involvement in writing this book is part of her development plan for this year. Last year she attended a number of development events, while this year she will spend more time in reflection and consolidation of learning.
» Working with a personal mentor and coach outside of the line-management relationship.

COST-JUSTIFYING TRAINING AND DEVELOPMENT

The only consistent approach to the issue of cost-justifying T&D is a pragmatic one. In some cases it is quite possible for a manager to look at a performance gap in a project team, for example, and show how its performance will improve in financial terms if training closes the gap. In other cases this will be very difficult. If, for example, a new member joins a team, it is sensible for them to go through the same team-working training as the team that they are joining has previously attended. It will be easier for them to communicate and work with other team members if they are familiar with the same jargon and processes; but how could you put a financial case for such an intervention?

Looked at this way, we can observe three types of return on investment from T&D.

1 *Productivity gains* – in Chapter 8 we mention research carried out in America that proved that education did have an effect on the productivity of the corporations in the study.

2 *Change-process benefits* – where teams or organizations are transforming the way they carry out their functions, it is possible to set objectives for the business benefits that flow from the change.

3 *Individual performance gains or individual productivity improvements* – where there is a direct link between a performance gap and the training intervention that closes the gap.

Here are some examples of these at the different levels in the model.

Organization level and the CEO's responsibility

There is scope here for massive gains to be made from initiatives such as quality improvement. Six Sigma, a set of statistical tools and processes aimed at reducing errors in processes to more or less zero, is a good case in point. If the board takes a decision, for example, to transform the delivery and distribution function in order to reduce defective products to almost zero, it will be easy to make a business case for this. The business case will include the cost of the training that will make up a considerable part of the costs of the project.

We can mention team-working and leadership development also at this level, which offers return on investment benefits in all three types; productivity, process change, and individual performance gaps.

AN EXAMPLE OF BENEFITS FLOWING FROM A CHANGE PROJECT

A company's sales force needed to change its style of selling from simply chasing high-volume product-oriented orders at competitive prices, into focusing on sales to the right customers that gave a better profit margin on sales. The training suite consisted of presentation skills, customer account management, and effective negotiation, all aimed at the clear outcome of not just more sales, but more profit.

After two years the profitability had gone up by a very significant amount.

Resource managed at the organization level, the HR responsibility

Mandatory training, however, will probably have to go under the productivity banner. Funding customer-care programs, complaint-handling procedures, fire safety, health and Safety is an essential part of top management's role, but is unlikely to form the basis for a financial case. However, when compared with the cost of failing in any of these areas, the training is plainly justified – just ask the insurance industry still reeling from the mis-selling of insurance policies caused by serious lapses in training and internal regulation.

There are ones in between productivity and process-change benefits, of course. Risk management training could make a significant contribution to profits if, as a result of the training, managers take more calculated risks, and take avoiding action to prevent risks occurring; but this will be difficult to estimate in advance.

HR are helpful in explaining the reflective type of training intervention. Are we capturing the experience of our people on a global basis, and making this available to others in the organization who will benefit from it? Does this reflectiveness lead to an expectation that employees and team leaders will be very development-and change-oriented in their approach to their job? It is not sufficient to do the job the way we did it yesterday any more. Everyone needs to be constantly looking towards the future and its changing demands. There is a productivity benefit here, or possibly in a competitive environment, a survival benefit.

Some people call this the learning organization, but we think this is a misnomer since the learning organization emerges as a result of doing things right. It is more an output and an indicator of effective organization performance. In the end the test is: can HR see a solid basis of learning clearly in the business plans, appraisal processes, and budget resource plans of the teams and departments?

As an aid to planning, here is a list grouping training interventions and proposing where the cost-justification may be found.

1 *Productivity gains through intervention to improve processes:*
   » meetings management
   » process redesign
   » problem solving
   » business plan development.
2 *Productivity gains and change-process benefits from mandatory interventions:*
   » health and safety
   » risk management
   » manual handling.
3 *Individual performance gains or individual productivity improvements from people-oriented interventions:*
   » managing poor performance
   » disciplinary procedures
   » appraisal
   » absence management.
4 *Change-process benefits from organizational culture interventions:*
   » induction
   » management development
   » team-working.

AN EXAMPLE OF BENEFITS FLOWING FROM AN HR INITIATIVE

A company had changed radically how it did business, in reaction to a major change in market expectations. The customer contact people were re-trained and in most cases reacted well, and tried to carry out their function in the new way. The problem lay with the supervisors of these people who still believed that the way they had acted would still lead to success. HR stepped in and put in place a program especially for the supervisor level that showed them what their people were being taught and explained what their role was in supporting their people to make the change. Since HR had put the infrastructure in place to deal with this, most supervisors were able to adapt to the new conditions and support their people in the new ways.

At departmental level

Modern processes rely on teamwork. This may be described as a strategic or productivity benefit, or it may be possible to isolate a business process; for example, in technology or project management, where the result of a teamwork intervention can be measured by the business benefits flowing from the improved process.

At departmental level the team leader pulls together plans for team and individual training. They then seek allocations from Levels 1 and 2 to meet these requirements.

Additional training requirements would be based on specific team or individual issues. A new idea at this level that is not served by the ideas and services available from the upper two levels has to be justified. At functional level there is frequently a technical content to this. Accountants, for example, have to attend a certain amount of training to keep their qualification to practice.

AN EXAMPLE OF BENEFITS FLOWING FROM A DEPARTMENTAL SPECIAL REQUEST

A new manager took over the men's departments of a major department store. Her brief was to restore sales in the department, which had fallen badly over the previous 12 months. She discovered that her predecessor had been maintaining profitability during the period of falling sales by taking on lower-paid staff with poor, if any, experience, and missing out on some maintenance projects in the store, and, amongst other things, training. The new manager discovered three main problems.

» Lack of maintenance had reduced the attractiveness of the floor area.
» Shop assistants were making this worse by paying little attention to clearing up after customers had disturbed products on the shelves and on the hangers.
» There was little or no attempt to cross-sell; that is, to ask a customer who, for example, had bought a shirt if they wanted to buy a tie.

Given as the desired outcome the restoration of sales volumes, the manager proposed measures to correct this, including the re-training of the whole floor. Management agreed to the budget and to the closure of the department for certain periods of time for training, and the shop assistants who were able to accept the change in how they were to behave quickly restored sales.

At individual level

Professional qualifications probably come within the productivity benefit item; but managers should not underestimate the value of retaining a person who would otherwise go to an employer who would fund such education.

But in the end, it is the closing of an individual performance gap on which the cost justification of training and development depends. And this brings us full circle, to the figure used in Chapter 1 (Fig. 6.1).

The closer managers have integrated objectives, performance measures, and training and development plans, the easier it will be to cost-justify the expenditure and defend the budget against all-comers.

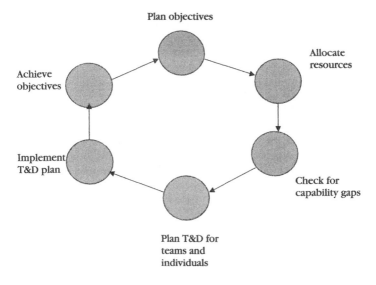

Fig. 6.1 The planning and training cycle.

AN EXAMPLE OF BENEFITS FLOWING FROM FILLING AN INDIVIDUAL PERFORMANCE GAP

A manager is brought into a health organization to manage a whole department. His experience had been on the nursing side, and he had been brought up to expect and use a military style of management (after all, nursing started in the Crimean War). This style was useless in managing and motivating therapists, doctors, and specialist clinicians. The training intervention was mainly off-site on training and coaching programs that explained and gave practice in different styles of leadership. After a short period of time the manager was able to adapt his style to one that was suitable for his new environment and allowed the team to hit its performance targets.

USING A RETURN-ON-INVESTMENT MODEL

Introduction

If managers have decided to justify expenditure on training and development in the same way as, say, managers are expected to cost-justify capital expenditure on buildings, plant, and materials, then they should become proficient with a comprehensive return-on-investment template (RoI). Here follows a state-of-the-art example, held electronically so that successful uses of it are made available to other people facing a similar financial challenge. In Chapter 7 there is an example of this tool in use to prove the return on investment of a training project.

Purpose (why)

To get a financial indicator of the return on investment of a project, in order to compare one project with any other.

Principles

» Using this model gives a consistent measure and makes sure that you are comparing like with like.
» The tool takes into account the relative riskiness of the project for comparison purposes.
» The tool points out where extra effort may be required to make sure that the financial objectives of the project are achieved.
» The tool eventually reduces every project to a single comparable number.

Application (how)

Figure 6.2 shows the model itself.

Table 6.1 illustrates the use of the RoI template. Enter first the reference material.

RETURN ON INVESTMENT

Name	
Team	
Date	
Status	

TITLE

SUMMARY

REFERENCE	DESCRIPTION
Project description	
Tax rate	
Discount factor	
Depreciation rate	
Asset residual value	

RISK PROFILE

REFERENCE	DESCRIPTION	RISK PROFILE
Type		
Novelty		
NPV dependency		
Cost criticality		
Time criticality		
Overall risk percentage		

Risk profile chart: R1, R2, R3, R4, R5 axes with scale 0, 0.2, 0.4, 0.6, 0.8, 1

SCENARIO	SITUATION DESCRIPTION
A-W	Worst case
A-E	Expected
A-B	Best case

SCENARIO		NPV	YEAR 0	YEAR 1	YEAR 2	YEAR 3	POST
PV-W	Worst case	£0	£0	£0	£0	£0	£0
PV-E	Expected	£0	£0	£0	£0	£0	£0
PV-B	Best case	£0	£0	£0	£0	£0	£0

PRESENT VALUES

Chart: NPV | Invest | Cashflows
Y-axis: £1, £1, £1, £1, £1, £1, £0, £0, £0, £0, £0
Legend: Worst case, Expected, Best csae
X-axis: NPV, YEAR 0, YEAR 1, YEAR 2, YEAR 3, POST

TD Finance.xls figures.xls Page 1 of 2

Fig. 6.2 Return on investment (RoI) template.

		FORECASTS	YEAR 0	YEAR 1	YEAR 2	YEAR 3	POST
WORST CASE	B1	Cost reduction/avoidance					
	B2	Revenue growth					
	B3	Capital expenditure					
	C1	Operating costs					
	C2	Operating cashflow	£0	£0	£0	£0	
	V1	Tax			£0	£0	£0
	V2	Tax - capital allowances			£0	£0	£0
	V3	Residual value				£0	
	V4	Cashflow	£0	£0	£0	£0	£0
	V5	Present value	£0	£0	£0	£0	£0
	V6	Net present value (NPV)	£0				

		FORECASTS	YEAR 0	YEAR 1	YEAR 2	YEAR 3	POST
EXPECTED	B1	Cost reduction/avoidance					
	B2	Revenue growth					
	B3	Capital expenditure					
	C1	Operating costs					
	C2	Operating cashflow	£0	£0	£0	£0	
	V1	Tax			£0	£0	£0
	V2	Tax - capital allowances			£0	£0	£0
	V3	Residual value				£0	
	V4	Cashflow	£0	£0	£0	£0	£0
	V5	Present value	£0	£0	£0	£0	£0
	V6	Net present value (NPV)	£0				

		FORECASTS	YEAR 0	YEAR 1	YEAR 2	YEAR 3	POST
BEST CASE	B1	Cost reduction/avoidance					
	B2	Revenue growth					
	B3	Capital expenditure					
	C1	Operating costs					
	C2	Operating cashflow	£0	£0	£0	£0	
	V1	Tax			£0	£0	£0
	V2	Tax - capital allowances			£0	£0	£0
	V3	Residual value				£0	
	V4	Cashflow	£0	£0	£0	£0	£0
	V5	Present value	£0	£0	£0	£0	£0
	V6	Net present value (NPV)	£0				

TD Finance.xls figures.xls Page 2 of 2

Fig. 6.2 (*continued*)

Table 6.1 Using the RoI template.

Group	No.	Reference	Description	
Summary	S1	Project description	A short description of the project.	
	S2	Tax rate	What is the marginal tax rate the tool should use for charging tax for increased profits and claiming allowances for expenditure? If you do not require to take tax into account, set this box to zero.	Do not put in the percentage sign, since the model is set to regard this number as a percentage.
	S3	Discount factor	What is the rate of return the project is required to exceed? This may be a standard for the organization. As long as a consistent rate is used the RoI tool will make a relevant comparison amongst projects. You may have to revisit this after you have done a risk analysis on the project. Managers generally expect a high-risk project to offer a higher rate of return than a low-risk one. Take account of this when setting this "hurdle" discount factor.	Rule of thumb. If inflation is at 3%, a discount factor of 7% would be a low-returning project, 12% a good return and anything over 20% an excellent return. Be careful, though, this rule of thumb is different for different industries.

(continued overleaf)

Table 6.1 (*continued*)

Group	No.	Reference	Description	
	S4	Depreciation rate	Enter the annual depreciation rate. Do not put in the percentage sign, since the model is set to regard this number as a percentage.	The tool uses this to calculate the tax cashflow. It allows tax against this depreciation rate in each of the three years of the project.
	S5	Residual value percentage	At the end of three years some expenditure on capital items may have a residual value. What is the percentage residual value at the end of the three-year project analysis? If it will have no value, set this box to zero.	Your organization may have a rule for this. If it will be the amount not written off in depreciation, you will have to work out what this figure should be; e.g. if depreciation is set at 25%, then the unwritten-down percentage will be 25%, which is what you should enter here.

Table 6.1 (*continued*)

Risk profile	R1	Type		

What is the predominant type of benefit from this project = cost reduction (least risky), cost avoidance (middle risk), or revenue growth (most risky)?

When looking at the benefits of an investment, generally speaking there is much less risk in achieving cost reductions and cost avoidance than revenue growth. If the project is mainly concerned with cost reduction you should set the risk indicator, the next column, fairly low. If the benefits are mainly concerned with avoiding costs that would occur if this project were not implemented, mark the risk medium. If all the benefits are concerned with growing revenues, then it is a high-risk project and should be marked as such.

Each of these risks is set an indicator from 1 to 10, where 1 is very low risk and 10 is extremely high.

(*continued overleaf*)

Table 6.1 (*continued*)

Group	No.	Reference	Description
	R2	Novelty	How novel are the activities involved in carrying out this project? a – routine b – modification to existing project c – new type of project. If the project is a repeat of things the organization has done before then it is a low risk. If the organization has operated in a similar way before then mark the risk medium. If this project is entirely new, then mark the risk high.
	R3	NPV dependency	At what level of business case must this project give the appropriate NPV? a – must pass on worst-case assumptions b – must pass on expected assumptions c – must pass on best-case assumptions. There are three levels of assumptions in the tool if you choose to use them. Worst-case assumptions describe the worst case in terms of the benefits. Expected are your best estimates of what is most likely actually to occur, and best-case is the best you could hope for.

Table 6.1 (*continued*)

If there are also different levels of risk on costs, then do the two exercises separately. That is, take the expected level of benefits and compare it with the three levels of costs. Otherwise, take the expected level of costs and compare them against the three levels of benefits.

If the project is required to achieve its RoI rate on the worst-case level of benefits, mark the project low-risk. If it is required to achieve the expected level of benefits then mark it as medium-risk, and if it can go ahead on the best-case benefits mark it as high-risk. You may also combine the estimates. For example, if you combine the worst-case costs and benefits, you get the overall worst case.

(*continued overleaf*)

Table 6.1 (continued)

Group No.	Reference	Description
R4	Cost criticality	How cost-critical is the project? a – budgets are not important b – budgets are normal c – budgets are very tight. How critical is it that the project remains within its budget? If there is easy access to more funds, mark it as low risk. If some more money could be made available, mark it as medium. If there is absolutely no further money available, mark it as high-risk.
R5	Time criticality	How time-critical is the project? a – timing is not important b – timing is of normal importance c – timing is a tight window of opportunity. If there is plenty of slippage time available, mark this as low. If it is important that this project is completed in time, then mark it medium. If there is a window of time available that must be achieved, mark this as high-risk

Table 6.1 (continued)

			If the overall percentage risk is around 50 you have a medium-risk project, well above 50 is high and well below is low. If the risk is extreme in either direction you may care to review the discount factor that the project must beat.
Assumptions	A-W	Worst case	On what assumptions have you based the worst-case scenario? Describe the possibilities here.
	A-E	Expected case	On what assumptions have you based the expected-case scenario? Describe the possibilities here.
	A-B	Best case	On what assumptions have you based the best-case scenario? Describe the possibilities here.

(continued overleaf)

Table 6.1 (*continued*)

Group	No.	Reference	Description
Present values	PV-W	Worst case	These represent the present value of the cashflows year by year for the worst case. The total value, the single number that you can use for comparison, is called the Net Present Value or NPV.
	PV-E	Expected case	These represent the present value of the cashflows year by year for the expected case. The total value, the single number that you can use for comparison, is called the Net Present Value or NPV.
	PV-B	Best case	These represent the present value of the cashflows year by year for the best case. The total value, the single number that you can use for comparison, is called the Net Present Value or NPV.

Table 6.1 (*continued*)

Each of the three cases			
	B1	Benefits Cost reduction and avoidance	What is the amount of cost that you are expending at the moment that will be saved through the implementation of this project? What costs that would occur if you do not implement this project, would this project avoid?
	B2	Benefits Revenue growth	What additional revenues will occur as a result of implementing this project?
	C1	Cost	What capital expenditure does the implementation of this project require?	You may find that there are specific rules in your organization to distinguish capital expenditure on this line from revenue expenditure on C1 in years 1,2, and 3.
	C2	Cost	What are the continuing running costs of this project?
	C3	Operating cashflow	The tool calculates the year-by-year cashflow of this project.

(*continued overleaf*)

Table 6.1 (*continued*)

Group	No.	Reference	Description	
	V1	Tax	Using the tax rate you gave at S3, the tool charges tax on the benefits of the project and allows tax against capital and revenue expenditure.	If you have set S3 at 0, then the tool will ignore all tax considerations.
	V2	Tax – capital allowances	The tool calculates tax allowances on capital expenditure as the capital value minus the residual value times the depreciation rate times the tax rate.	You may have to check that this is relevant for your organization.
	V3	Residual value	The tool calculates the residual value from the percentage you gave at S5 and puts this in as a positive cashflow item at year 3.	
	V4	Cashflow	This is the year-by-year cashflow of the project.	

Table 6.1 (*continued*)

V5	Present value	This is the present value of the cashflows discounted by the factor you entered in S4.
V6	Net present value	This is a cross-add of the present values to give the net present value. If this figure is positive it means that the project does meet the rate of return in S4. If it is negative it does not meet that rate.
		The higher this number is, the better the RoI. This is the single number you can use to compare financially one project with another.

Note: the items for B1 to V6 have the same definition for the three cases – worst, expected, and best.

Managing Training and Development Finance in Practice

This chapter details the steps involved in proving the financial worth of T&D by considering:

» a case study of a service organization seeking to redirect the HR team and improve the HR contribution to the company;
» using the return on investment (RoI) model to justify a major change project; and
» using interventions to ensure projects achieve their objectives.

CASE 1 – IMPROVING THE TEAMWORK OF AN EXISTING TEAM

A director of HR reviewed the role and performance of her department. The department had a poor reputation in the organization, was overstretched, and had been recently reorganized. She had clarified the HR role in the organization and identified the key service areas to focus on over the next two years. Her main thrust was to move from an administrative policing personnel function, to a consultancy service with specialist expertise to support line managers in recruiting and managing their people. The HR director was clear that only so much could be done through redirecting the effort of the department, restructuring it and improving the technical competence of the team. The resource profile was very tight and poor team-working meant that flexibility, cover, responsiveness, and general productivity were not high enough.

Her solution was to invest time and money in T&D over a 12-month period to improve team functioning.

The process

The HR director took as a starting point that she would be able to win FD support for training investment by taking a confident line, emphasizing the strategic importance of the change. She demonstrated a clear departmental strategy, owned and understood by her director peer-group and fitted into the organization's strategy.

She could also demonstrate rigorous financial management and cost savings achieved over the previous two years during various restructuring and savings programs. She could show how the team-working program fitted in with other development approaches, her performance management of the directorate, and how she would follow up and integrate the training program's outputs into her management of the directorate. The time had come, she claimed, to invest in the teams' working environment and capabilities.

Generally speaking, team-working sessions go better with a facilitator, from outside the department certainly, and ideally from outside the organization. Managers should expect at this time some resistance from some managers and plan accordingly; so next in the process was selecting an external facilitator. This should be a rigorous task since the success of the person in selling themselves to the team and getting their trust is an important ingredient in making such sessions work.

She now knew the cost of her plan and asked for the budget. In a later case study we will show how a manager can in some circumstances build a line-by-line business case justifying the expenditure, but in this case demonstrating that it was obviously the right course of action for the team and the organization more or less made the financial issue a non-issue. If you are getting the management of your department right, it becomes easier and easier to get the finance to support your change and capability building plans.

Next the HR director ensured that the program and its aims were reflected in individuals' personal development plans, even in those of managers who showed a certain skepticism about team-working sessions which they rather rudely described as "contemplating the team's navel."

The performance deficit

Senior managers and the team agreed the performance deficit as follows.

» The HR function was slow to respond to functional managers' requests for information and advice.
» Where functional managers depended on HR for administrative tasks they found they were also done slowly.
» Managers complained that the HR service was inflexible and unable to cope with, for example, the problems of recruiting rare IT specialists in a seller's market.
» HR was geared to cater for different HR service imperatives than were needed in the field.
» The expert advice from HR was poor and sometimes dangerously out-of-date.
» Overall, the service HR was providing had little quantifiable or unquantifiable impact on improving the performance of the organization, or the performance of the organization in recruiting, training, and developing its people.

The desired outcomes

Senior managers and the team decided to use a before-and-after questionnaire filled in by the customers (the functional managers) to set some of the actual targets, and agreed the desired outcomes as follows.

» Speed of response improvement measured by the questionnaires.
» High quality administrative processes measured by gaining ISO 9000 approval.
» Up-to-date high-quality service measured by acceptance by Investors in People membership.
» Confident consultancy and professional performance of the team and its individuals measured by the appraisals of the team and its leader.
» The performance of line managers in taking responsibility for their own people would be measured by their use of and adherence to the appraisal and personal development planning of their people.
» Clear objectives leading to team members focusing on following through tasks to completion, and a huge reduction in crises and firefighting measured by the departmental plan, showing much more activity in areas that had a high impact on the business with low urgency, and less in areas of high impact and high urgency.

The program plan

Table 7.1 is the program plan, with priorities set in terms of impact and urgency using high, medium, and low. The team carried out the plan and met all of the desired outcomes set within the extra budget agreed for this strategic project.

CASE 2 – USING THE RETURN ON INVESTMENT MODEL ON A MAJOR CHANGE PROJECT

The performance deficit

A company has a problem in its distribution and delivery service. At the moment deliveries are made to customers correctly; that is, on time and requiring no corrections between 60% and 70% of the time. Definition of the problem shows a major behavior problem in the sales force,

Table 7.1 Program plan.

Priority		Key capability development	How	Outcome	By when
Impact	Urgency				
H	M	Strategic management capability within the team	Strategy process and communications skills	Clear understanding of role of function and of individuals within team. Confidence in communicating this.	In 1 year
H	H	Customer relationship management skills	Training program and process skills	Processes for engaging and disengaging with customers effectively, setting expectations and delivering against these.	3 months
H	H	High-level team performance	Workshops – facilitated	Flexible, interchangeable team, able to cover and support each other. Learning environment.	Start in 3 months

(continued overleaf)

Table 7.1 (continued)

Priority		Key capability development	How	Outcome	By when
Impact	Urgency				
H	M	Presentation skills	Training program	Credible proposals and formal interventions that improve organizational performance.	1 year
H	L	Professional development, updating and accreditation	Professional qualifications an updating	Accredited status, credentials as consultants, improved confidence as practitioners.	3 years
H	M	Problem identification and resolution skills	Training program	Process skills to improve and direct quality of HR technical expertise.	6 months
H	M	Being an effective internal consultant	Training program and reflective practice within the team	Consciousness of the nature of their interventions with other human beings, being aware of the full impact of the role of a consultant to concentrate on continuously improving performance.	1 year

and a disconnection between the sales function and the production department. This leads to salespeople setting wrong expectations at their customers, either because the benefits the product offers will not fulfill their expectation, or the functionality of the product does not meet the expected specification, or simply because it is not possible for the company to organize delivery at the time the customer expects.

The desired outcome

By comparing its performance with others in the same industry and with available benchmarks, the company sets, somewhat artificially, a target of improving correct deliveries to between 90% and 95% of the time. This is a difficult number to estimate, being difficult to know whether it is achievable or whether they could in the event do even better; but the target is acceptable because it is made an imperative by external pressures of the competition.

The program

The change project in the main depends on getting three things right:

» improve the communication, team-working, and mutual respect of the sales force and the production team;
» improve the process by which the sales force agrees at what level to set customer expectations; and
» train and motivate the sales force to use the process consistently and rigidly.

The emphasis of the program is therefore team-working and training, and the HR department is put in charge of the cross-functional change project.

Estimating the benefits

This is perhaps the most difficult part of the estimating process. As we have seen, it often has an emotional overtone with managers who are making the estimates aware that they will turn into increased targets or stiffer objectives if the expenditure is approved. It is useful for estimating reasons, and also for risk analysis as we will see, to break the benefits into three categories:

» increases in revenue;
» reduction in costs; and
» avoidance of future costs.

Let's take these one at a time.

Increases in revenue

The top line of any proposed profit and loss account is sales. This is true whether the sales are external, to the company's customers, or internal to other departments within the business. Expenditure of money will often have as the first part of the justification claims that revenues will increase.

Most times when estimating revenues you will need to use a range of results. The most common method of doing this is to take three possibilities:

» pessimistic – the lowest outcome that you believe possible;
» most likely – your view of what will actually happen; and
» optimistic – the best, but still feasible, outcome.

In our example the increases in revenue are simple to identify but difficult to quantify. HR decides to look at a number of customers where difficulties with deliveries are causing real pain, and the threat of losing business to the competition. They ask sales for their estimates of what the increases in revenue from the improved delivery performance might be. Table 7.2 shows what they come up with.

From this they can calculate three possibilities for the total increase in revenue stream. This will be the basis for the projected profit and loss account in the business case. The pessimistic case assumes that only the prospects in likelihood 1 will place an order. The most likely case adds the prospects in likelihood 2, and the optimistic assumes all the prospects will come on board (see Table 7.3).

Reduction in costs

Finance people are likely to agree that a reduction of costs is the most tangible benefit there is. There is reduction in costs in terms of savings of returned products for modification, and engineers' time to go and modify or repair products. These are estimated below.

Table 7.2   Revenue estimates.

	Customer	Year 1	Years 2 and 3
Likelihood 1	Customer A	112	150
	Customer B	162	324
	Customer C	90	120
	Customer D	36	48
	Customer E	0	158
Total Likelihood 1		400	800
Likelihood 2	Customer F	112	70
	Customer G	64	82
	Customer H	24	48
Total Likelihood 2		200	200
Likelihood 3	Customer I	60	120
	Customer J	40	80
Total Likelihood 3		100	200

Table 7.3   Summary of revenue estimates.

Year	1	2	3
Pessimistic (Likelihood 1)	400	800	800
Most likely (Likelihood 1 + 2)	600	1,000	1,000
Optimistic (Likelihood 1 + 2 + 3)	700	1,200	1,200

Avoidance of future costs

The avoidance of future costs is a slightly different concept from a straightforward reduction in costs. This brings into the business case for a project costs which would be incurred if the project were not undertaken. There are none in this project.

Table 7.4   Estimate of project costs.

Year	1	2	3
Consultancy	50		
Training	56	101	92
IT processing costs	40	80	90
	146	181	182

Estimating the costs

In comparison with benefits, costs are more straightforward to estimate. There is major capital expenditure cost for computer equipment that HR gets directly from the internal supplier of IT services.

The operating costs are agreed as shown in Table 7.4.

Figure 7.1 shows the model filled in for the project proposal. This model is introduced and explained in detail in Chapter 6 (The State of the Art). Since the NPV dependency was set at the expected case, we can assume that this case passes the hurdle rate of return with its expected case NPV at £281,000 positive. That does not of itself make the decision for managers. They have then to look at the strategic fit of the project, and senior managers may well look at other ways in which they could invest the money. All in all, the HR department has put the organization into a strong position to make a decision on this change project.

It is salutary to notice how well this project is presented in the context of the business performance. If HR had attempted to show the benefits of this in terms of productivity, or in terms of the filling of individual performance deficits, cost-justification would have been much harder. As it is, the project mainly gets its benefits from changes to some internal processes, and therefore proves a good rate of return through the better performance of the business. This linkage of HR deriving a training and development plan starting from the objectives and strategies of the business is further illustrated in Chapter 10 (Ten Steps to Managing Training and Development Finance).

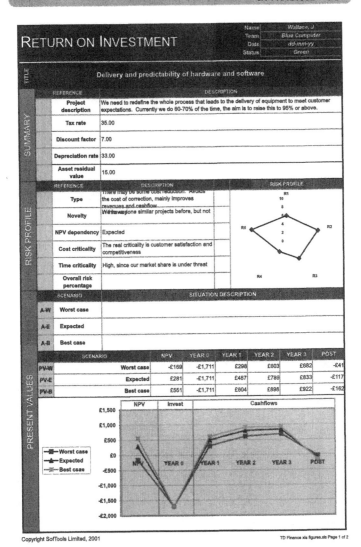

Fig. 7.1 Return on investment (RoI) calculation.

WORST CASE

	FORECASTS	YEAR 0	YEAR 1	YEAR 2	YEAR 3	POST
B1	Cost reduction/avoidance		£65	£15	£15	
B2	Revenue growth		£400	£800	£800	
B3	Capital expenditure	£1,711				
C1	Operating costs		£146	£181	£182	
C2	Operating cashflow	-£1,711	£319	£634	£633	
V1	Tax			-£112	-£222	-£222
V2	Tax - capital allowances			£168	£168	£168
V3	Residual value				£267	
V4	Cashflow	-£1,711	£319	£690	£836	-£54
V5	Present value	-£1,711	£288	£603	£602	-£41
V6	Net present value (NPV)	-£169				

EXPECTED

	FORECASTS	YEAR 0	YEAR 1	YEAR 2	YEAR 3	POST
B1	Cost reduction/avoidance		£67	£99	£99	
B2	Revenue growth		£800	£1,000	£1,000	
B3	Capital expenditure	£1,711				
C1	Operating costs		£146	£181	£182	
C2	Operating cashflow	-£1,711	£521	£918	£917	
V1	Tax			-£182	-£321	-£321
V2	Tax - capital allowances			£168	£168	£168
V3	Residual value				£257	
V4	Cashflow	-£1,711	£521	£904	£1,020	-£153
V5	Present value	-£1,711	£487	£789	£833	-£117
V6	Net present value (NPV)	£281				

BEST CASE

	FORECASTS	YEAR 0	YEAR 1	YEAR 2	YEAR 3	POST
B1	Cost reduction/avoidance		£92	£67	£67	
B2	Revenue growth		£700	£1,200	£1,200	
B3	Capital expenditure	£1,711				
C1	Operating costs		£146	£181	£182	
C2	Operating cashflow	-£1,711	£646	£1,086	£1,085	
V1	Tax			-£226	-£380	-£380
V2	Tax - capital allowances			£168	£168	£168
V3	Residual value				£257	
V4	Cashflow	-£1,711	£646	£1,028	£1,130	-£212
V5	Present value	-£1,711	£604	£898	£922	-£162
V6	Net present value (NPV)	£551				

Fig. 7.1 (*continued*)

CASE 3 – A CAUTIONARY TALE

The only certainty about an IT implementation is that the jobs of some people are going to change. Most large organizations are getting better at managing such change. There are, however, still some, along with many smaller businesses, who handle this part of the process at best insufficiently, and at worst with a lack of sensitivity. This imperils the success of the project.

In this case we study an IT project that went badly wrong, and discover that the management of a High Street supermarket had failed to recognize the early need to involve and engage store managers, and the staff who would have their jobs changed as a result of the project. The cure belongs in the training budget, although it does not replace the technical training needed as well. The development of the people involved brings them to an understanding of the benefits of change to their company, their customers, and themselves.

A large supermarket chain was replacing outdated checkout equipment with the latest in Electronic Point of Sale (EPOS) hardware and software. The chain in question had some 200 sites in the UK, and had the intention of introducing advanced EPOS, first in a pilot site, and then throughout the group.

Senior management agreed challenging project objectives:

» to reduce time at checkout and improve customer satisfaction;
» to improve stock control and shelf-stocking activity;
» to improve the productivity of checkout operators; and
» to improve job satisfaction both in the front-of-store and back-of-store areas.

Given the volumes, margins, and stock sensitivities of a supermarket, all the objectives were easy to build into a business case. Senior management recognized that the project would add many millions of pounds to the bottom line.

The IT people chose hardware and software, and used the supplier's people to train the operators of the equipment and the in-store users of the new information. The training concentrated on keystrokes, error messages, the process of serving a customer, and so on. Engineers installed the equipment and saw it through its acceptance tests. The suppliers did the training, in the case of the pilot site, just after they had installed the equipment, and just before the project went live. Management looked forward to the results.

In fact the pilot was a disaster. Every single objective area produced a negative result. The queues were longer and shelf-stocking actually got worse.

» Customers' frustration made them act out in fact the store manager's nightmare – they abandoned full trolleys near the checkouts. The process of replacing these items on the shelves is almost as expensive as throwing the whole lot away.
» Staff members were so upset that key and long-serving people were leaving or threatening to do so.

What had gone wrong? The resulting post mortem drew the conclusion that it was the early stage of the project that had misfired. The people in the stores were unaware of what was actually happening, although fully aware that their normal way of life was about to undergo a major upheaval.

The implementation managers found a simple solution. During the build-up to each store installing advanced EPOS, local management arranged a series of activities guided by a package of material developed centrally. Thus, store managers received a box of materials. Instructions helped them to put posters up at appropriate times, signaling the approach of the new technology. Store managers distributed newspapers with information on advanced EPOS, including crosswords and competitions that added some interest. There was no central trainer intervention since local managers had the materials to carry out the exercise themselves. It was like a live team-working exercise.

By the time technical training was due, staff were comfortable with the concept and actively looking forward to their role in the implementation. The implementation proceeded smoothly and management could see the business benefits coming clearly through on to the bottom line. Not only that, but in the event the number of people involved with training diminished from the plan and the simple process paid for itself time and time again as an avoidance of cost.

In its original conception the project carried a huge and more or less unrecognized risk – the rejection of the new processes by the people involved. What needs to be in place to make sure that such a situation does not occur, by spending the necessary money at the right time?

» IT managers and others involved in changing processes must realize that the impact on people is probably the biggest hurdle to the change that they will have to jump, and stop and think about this, before proceeding.
» Managers supported by HR people must be deeply involved early on in change projects to look for the development requirements and identify the correct interventions.
» Senior management must be prepared to agree budgets for training and development where the business case is the mitigation of any risk that will have a major impact on the success of a project or of the organization itself.
» HR people need to look laterally at what interventions are necessary to find the simplest and most cost-effective solution to a problem or potential problem. They do this by understanding the objectives that the business is pursuing as well as the activities that it is about to put in place.

KEY LEARNING POINTS

» If senior managers, including finance managers, are sure that what your department is doing is strategic to the organization, and the department is well run, they will tend to agree a well-argued program of training as part of the strategic requirement of the organization.
» When training is directly involved with changing a basic business process, managers should be able to find the business benefits of introducing the change and cost-justify it accordingly.
» If the people who have to accept a change in how they work are not brought into a change process early, you run a high risk that the expected return on investment will not occur.

Key Concepts and Thinkers

The main part of this chapter describes the key words and concepts used in the topic:

» useful and usable performance measurement indicators;
» education and training as productivity tools; and
» training in areas such as leadership and teamwork as strategic disciplines.

It also provides a glossary of terms.

MAKING THE MOST OF THE T&D BUDGET

We have noted, in Chapter 2 (Definition of Terms), the opinion of many thinkers and writers on training and development that much of the T&D budget is wasted. There are three issues that contribute towards this, and leading thinkers are active in all three.

» When we measure performance for management control purposes, never mind T&D, are we measuring the right numbers and making sensible decisions based on sensible indicators?
» How do we show the connection between training, education, and productivity?
» What is the payback in improving teamwork?

Tony Hope and Jeremy Hope

In their book *Transforming the Bottom Line* (Nicholas Brealey Publishing Limited, 1995), the authors challenge the first of these three concepts by pointing out that many of the traditional ways of putting in key indicators to measure financial performance have little to do with the actual impact that the activity of the people in the business are having on the product or service that is delivered to the customer. They argue that figures that flow up and down the organization are poor indicators of who is generating value and where are they doing it.

They use simple examples, such as the often ludicrous way that overheads are added to internal profit and loss accounts, actively discouraging the managers from doing business in those cases where overheads are allocated against revenues. Indeed, Ken, one of the authors of this book, has a brilliant case in point. A small company in a particular niche wanted to buy the division of a large company that was the leader of the niche market. The entrepreneurs that ran the small business had found out that the management accounting system the division had to work within was showing it making a loss of about £250,000 a year. By offering and paying £250,000 for the division the small business solved a number of problems for the large company – a number of managers improved their performance as measured by the internal accounting system. The following year the division, now part of the small company, showed a profit of more than £250,000 and the new managers had actually changed very little.

It was the management accounting system that was giving very poor information to management.

Hope and Hope advise companies to reform the way they measure performance by recognizing that the useful figures in an organization:

"... flow horizontally across functional boundaries, following the chain of the company's value-adding processes. They emphasize improvement rather than control. At their heart lies the key issue – the measurement of work – and the key question – does the work performed add value to the customer?"

They look at the actions that managers traditionally take to cost-cutting and find a vicious circle of declining profits, where cutting the workforce despite the work remaining the same leads to a lowering of morale, causing the best employees to leave. After they have gone, customer service suffers, orders decline, and profits fall. It is not hard to guess in this scenario what managers do next – they cut the workforce again. In our experience you can see exactly the same vicious circle by replacing "cutting the workforce" with "cutting training."

The book shows how to avoid this vicious circle, and gives as the key tasks of doing it:

» cut the workload not the workforce;
» manage performance with the real numbers;
» develop a horizontal team-based organization;
» align performance measures with strategy;
» sell profitable products and services;
» find and retain profitable customers; and
» implement a horizontal information system.

In one example they look at the activity profile of a salesperson, dividing the activities they are involved in into high relevance, such as negotiating and order-taking, down to low relevance, such as internal meetings. It is interesting to note that training activity comes in the top half of this relevance measure.

OK, so we have put in place a series of measures that highlight the areas where activity is adding value to the customer supply-chain.

How do we make sure that we can connect T&D activities to these new measures?

Henry Mintzberg

Let us redress the balance somewhat by looking at some sobering thoughts from a leading American thinker. In "Musings on Management" in the *Harvard Business Review* of July–August, 1996, Henry Mintzberg, a professor of management at INSEAD in Fontainebleau, France, and at McGill University in Canada, takes one or two surprising lines of argument that are very relevant to the T&D finance topic. Despite his positions, he advises us that we should close down conventional MBA programs.

Start from a challenge to bring to mind a few of the really good US chief executives, leaders who have made or are making a sustained difference, and then see which of them has an MBA. Most people find it easy to bring to mind Jack Welch and Bill Gates, neither of whom has bothered with a business school. One, Jack Welch, is highly educated and is a chemical engineer, while Gates did not finish a first degree.

Mintzberg pours scorn on people who attend business school and then expect to be parachuted into a middle manager's job in no matter what industry. Business schools, he says, are good at technical training for specialist jobs such as market research and financial analysis – neither of which have much to do with management. He argues that management is not a technical skill or a science or even an applied science, but rather it is a practice or a craft.

Parachuting MBAs into organizations, and giving them a fast track up the ladder without troubling them to get an intimate knowledge of what is going on below them, has to be folly since it puts such people in charge of those who, because of their experience, do have such an intimate knowledge. Mintzberg further criticizes the folly of the career-path MBA into consultancy with one of the world's majors, skipping from company to company, and then into running a business. His view is that some people may on occasion be successful in this way, but it is not a way to plan and build a strong competitive corporation.

Knowing how to work in one industry does not enable people to work in others, outside a narrow focus of knowledge and experience in such a discipline, say, as marketing, in any consumer products company. Gates and Welch, he points out, have devoted their careers to single companies.

OK, so that, in the opinion of Mr Mintzberg is how not to spend the T&D budget. What does he suggest we do? In the same article he talks about the difference between interventions by senior managers that are dramatic, often involve cutting things out, and radically altering their organizations in the hope of fixing them. His suggestion is that we look for ways to promote continuous care rather than interventionist cures, and continues this metaphor by talking about nursing as a good model for management, on the way implying that this means that women may in the end be seen to be much more effective managers than men (remembering that nursing is a profession dominated by women).

So what does a nursing-style manager do? Most noticeably they spend almost none of their time in their offices. Good nursing takes place in partnership with the patient on a continuous basis. Being at the sharp end is not a favored style of management, most people preferring one or two other styles: the *boss* style, showing the same care to employees as a nineteenth century mill-owner; or the popular *professional* style, where someone, probably an MBA, is known to know management and is therefore expected to be able to manage anything regardless of experience. Mintzberg describes this professional management as "management by remote control."

The third style, and his preferred nursing style, is the *craft* style of management. It is about inspiring people and showing leadership. It means getting involved enough to know when you should not be involved. It is very much a hands-on style of team leadership. Rather than talking about the glass ceiling, the craft style of management smashes up the concrete floors that prevent the people at the top knowing what is going on below them. He advocates more transparency in management.

Before drawing our conclusion from Mintzberg, let us take another view on this from an unlikely source as a key thinker.

In his autobiography *Writing Home*, the playwright Alan Bennett gives an insight into different attitudes amongst team members. He differentiates musicians from actors. In the first case:

"Striking about the musicians is their total absence of self-importance."

He describes how musicians play a piece and then discuss amongst themselves as to how it might be improved. They make suggestions to each other directly, not via the director. Anyone is invited to comment, their views noted and in some cases adopted when they go to repeat the piece. According to Bennett this would be impossible with actors.

"No actor would tolerate a fellow performer who ventured to comment on what he or she is doing – comment of that sort coming solely from the director, and even then it has to be carefully packaged and seasoned with plenty of love and appreciation,"

states Bennett.

This is just what it is in business. In most teams that have not consciously developed their team-working skills, the egos of the individuals get in the way of sharing suggestions. There are exceptions and they tend to be successful people and we should watch out for them. They encourage openness and constructive criticism of everyone, by everyone. They tend to be very laid-back, good listeners and very understanding of people's problems. When they are team members they are terrific allies of the team leader and still liked by their colleagues in the team. When they are team leaders they bring the best out of people continuously. They don't manage everyone in the same way, though, some of the team they can encourage to be musicians, and some will always be actors. You can develop good teams in the musicians' model. Good team leadership should be concentrating on the team's functioning as a core part of their job. This will require investment in training and development as well as good leadership.

Fiona, while managing a National Health Trust, actually observes what both these thinkers are helping us to understand. Effective healthcare professionals are increasingly, in her experience, seeking to reflect on their practice and explore openly what has been good and bad, to thirst for new knowledge from someone whose experience is different from theirs and to spend all their time at the point of provision of service. This goes for the whole healthcare team, where their success in this style of working has a major impact on the quality of service to the patient.

For those people whose natural style is not the craft or nursing style, we have to recognize a performance gap that must be filled. Strategically we can therefore easily recognize the need to spend money on developing and training leaders; tactically we have to work hard to see the operational return on this investment.

These current thinkers reinforce two of the main themes of this book – the need for T&D to be planned at the three levels of organization, teams and individuals, and the need to recognize training as a strategic contribution to the organization; well-connected to the organization's business plans and strategies with its measures of effectiveness based on actual business and personal performance.

GLOSSARY OF TERMS

Accounting policies – Those principles and practices applied by an entity that specify how the effects of transactions and other events are to be reflected in the accounts. For example, an entity may have a policy of revaluing fixed assets or of maintaining them at historical cost. Accounting policies do not include estimation techniques but will impact the presentation of business cases.

Accrual – An expense or a proportion thereof not yet invoiced.

Accruals concept – Income and expenses are recognized in the period in which they are earned or incurred, rather than the period in which they happen to be received or paid. This may impact the building of a business case.

Appraisal review – This is usually a follow-up to the annual appraisal on a quarterly basis or after six months, depending on the seniority and experience of the employee in the post. It is more a discussion on progress, following the same format of the annual appraisal, but part of the continuous performance improvement and feedback process that should be established by the effective supervisor.

Asset – Any property or rights owned by the company that have a monetary value. In UK accounting standards, assets are defined as "rights or other access to future economic benefits controlled by an entity as a result of past transactions or events."

Break-even analysis – A form of analysis that relates activity to totals of revenue and costs based on the classification of costs into fixed and variable.

Break-even point – The level of activity at which the fixed costs of a project are just covered by the contribution from sales. At this point there is neither a profit nor a loss.

Cashflow forecast – A statement of future, anticipated cash balances based on estimated cash inflows and outflows over a given period.

Costs of capital – The weighted average costs of funds to a company based on the mix of equity and loan capital and their respective costs. This is sometimes used as the required rate of return in a discounted cashflow.

Costs of goods sold (or cost of sales) – Those costs (usually raw materials, labor, and production overheads) directly attributable to goods that have been sold. The difference between sales and cost of goods sold is gross profit.

Culture – "The way we do things around here." People talk about developing the right organizational culture when it is clear that the way people behave and the values behind that behavior do not create an environment which supports an organization delivering its strategic imperatives.

Current cost – The convention by which assets are valued at the cost of replacement at the balance sheet date (net of depreciation for fixed assets).

Deferred taxation – An estimate of a tax liability payable at some estimated future date, resulting from timing differences in the taxation and accounting treatment of certain items of income and expenditure. In complex project financial estimating the timing of tax cashflows may have to be taken into account.

Depreciation – An estimate of the proportion of the cost of a fixed asset that has been consumed (whether through use, obsolescence, or the passage of time) during the accounting period.

Discounted cashflow (DCF) – This is a method of appraisal for investment projects. The total incremental stream of cash for a project is tested to assess the level of return it delivers to the investor. If the return exceeds the required, or hurdle, rate the project is recommended on financial terms, or vice versa.

EBIT – Earnings (profit) before interest and tax.

EBITDA – Earnings (profit) before interest, tax, depreciation, and amortization. This measure of operating cashflow is considered to be an important measure of the performance of a business entity.

Estimation techniques – The methods adopted by an organization to arrive at estimated monetary amounts for items in the accounts. For example, of the various methods that could be adopted for depreciation, the entity may select to depreciate using the straight-line method. This will impact the presentation of business cases.

Expense – A cost incurred, or a proportion of a cost, the benefit of which is wholly used up in the earning of the revenue for a particular accounting period.

Fixed asset – Asset held for use by the business rather than for sale.

Fixed cost – A cost that does not vary in proportion to changes in the scale of operations, e.g. rent.

Gross profit – The difference between sales and the cost of goods sold.

Historic cost convention – The convention by which assets are valued on the basis of the original cost of acquiring or producing them.

Hurdle rate – The rate of return decided on by a company as the minimum acceptable for capital investment. It will be governed by the company's cost of capital and it may allow for different levels of risk.

Internal rate of return (IRR) – The rate of discount that brings the present value of all the cashflows associated with a capital investment to zero. It measures the effective yield on the investment. If this yield is greater than the hurdle rate the investment is seen to be financially desirable, and vice versa.

Leadership – Taking people from A to B by ensuring clarity about what needs to be done by an organization, department, or individual employee; ensuring the environment, climate, or culture supports delivery of this task by showing this clarity of purpose, and modeling the values and behaviors you expect of people.

Liability – An amount owed. In UK accounting standards, liabilities are defined as "an entity's obligations to transfer economic benefits as a result of past transactions or events."

Net assets – The amount of total assets less total liabilities.

Net book value – The cost (or valuation) of fixed assets less accumulated depreciation to date. Net book value bears no relationship to market value.

Net present value (NPV) – A positive or negative value arrived at by discounting the cashflow from a capital project by the desired rate of return. If the value is positive, it means that the project is desirable, and vice versa.

Net realizable value – Amount at which an asset could be sold in its existing condition at a specific date, after deducting any costs to be incurred in disposing of it.

Opportunity cost – The alternative advantage foregone as a result of the commitment of resources to one particular end.

Overhead – Any expense, other than the direct cost of materials or labor involved, in making a company's products.

Payback period – A term used in investment appraisal. It refers to the time required for the non-discounted cash inflow to accumulate to the initial cash outflow in the investment.

Performance appraisal – Usually once a year – a formal discussion between supervisor and employee to agree the level and quality of performance over the past year, by reference to the job the employee is required to do as defined in their job description. It takes note of specific objectives during the past 12 months, and key changes and developments in the environment the employee has performed their job within. An effective appraisal is a mutual discussion, where the employee knows all the issues to be discussed (no surprises). The employee should lead the discussion and the supervisor, who also provides appropriate and constructive performance feedback, should act as a facilitator. The annual discussion will also cover future career goals and personal development plans.

Personal development plan – A PDP should be part of the formal annual appraisal, and formulated from the appraisal discussion on performance improvements and developments that can be made to enable the employee to perform their job, deliver objectives and respond to change effectively. A PDP will also address future career aspirations that the supervisor and employee have agreed they should support. Usually a PDP will describe the nature of development outcome required, the type of activity needed to deliver it with an indication of potential cost, and whether the employee or supervisor will take responsibility for the activity.

Price/earnings ratio – The relationship between the market price of a share and its latest reported earnings per share. This is connected to the expected rate of return that the board will expect from the projects that T&D managers are proposing.

Profit – The difference between the revenues earned in the period and the costs incurred in earning them. Alternative definitions are possible according to whether the figure is struck before or after tax.

Profit and loss account – A statement summarizing the revenues and the costs incurred in earning them during an accounting period.

Residual value – A notional cash inflow attributed to a capital project to allow for value remaining in the project at the final year of the assessment.

Revenue – Money received from selling the product of the business.

Sensitivity analysis – Analysis of the change in the output values of an equation by small changes to the input values. It is used to assess the risk in an investment project.

Teams – Groups of individuals who work together on a piece of work that may be a time-limited project, running an organization or department, or service delivery/product development function.

Teamwork – How groups of individuals functioning, interacting, processing information together perform.

Training interventions – These are formal events outside of the normal job activity of an individual or team, designed to improve or develop the skills of an individual or team. Facilitated team away-days, formal training courses, conferences, qualifications are all training interventions.

Turnover – Revenue from sales.

Variable cost – A cost that increases or decreases in line with changes in the level of activity.

Working capital – Current assets less current liabilities, representing the amount a business needs to invest – and which is continually circulating – in order to finance its stock, debtors, and work-in-progress.

KEY LEARNING POINTS

» The best performance measures that can be used as a measure also of investment in T&D are those concerned with the activities that add value to the customer offering.

» While future estimates of the productivity improvement to be gained from education may be difficult, there is research that says it has been effective in this area in the past.

» Investing in team-working training and development is a given in any successful organization nowadays.

» The T&D plan is most effectively used in an environment where management is seen as a craft rather than a science.

Resources

This chapter refers to books, Websites, and other publications relevant to the T&D finance topic.

BOOKS

We have picked out five books that Fiona has found particularly helpful in developing her knowledge of training and development, and their management.

John Kenney & Margaret Reid, *Training Interventions*, Institute of Personnel Management, 1986

Training Interventions gives an overview of the main issues in training and contains many useful references for those wishing to study aspects in more depth. Beginning with a consideration of the nature of training and its organizational role – the organization is seen as a powerful learning environment, and training is regarded as a deliberate intervention in this book – the book continues with the assessment of organizational and individual needs, and the planning and evaluation of training strategies. The authors consider issues in the training of young people and adults, and the book concludes with a chapter on the evolving national training scene.

Nick Georgiades & Richard Macdonell, *Leadership for Competitive Advantage*, Wiley, 1998

For those people involved in transforming their organization, this book balances academic knowledge with practical experience. It answers the real and complex needs of leaders attempting to balance the seemingly conflicting demands of a turbulent external environment and the needs of the shareholders, customers, and employees.

The book outlines an interesting "Model of Organizational Effectiveness" that is a guide to sorting and assigning priorities for action. It enumerates the key steps in the process of making significant change, and offers hints and practical advice to help the reader on his or her individual journey. Fiona has found this model very useful in conveying her views on the complexity of, and therefore the care needed in, implementing effective organizational change.

Jeremy Hope & Tony Hope, *Competing in the Third Wave*, Harvard Business School Press, 1997

This book considers the problems in getting managers to look positively at training as an investment rather than a cost that can be cut. Their argument starts from the fact that the third wave is the technological deluge of information now available to managers and professionals like researchers, software engineers, accountants, doctors, and teachers - the knowledge managers of the modern workforce.

They say that education and training has an obvious connection with productivity, but because accounting systems see it as a periodic expense, managers are actually motivated to minimize its cost. Worse, many managers in this area regard training as a threat - if I train these people they become more valuable and therefore more likely to be poached by a rival organization.

What we ought to do is measure the productivity of knowledge workers by the amount of time they spend in their specialist work. The authors cite the example of doctors who are involved in more and more administration, supervision, and filling out of regulatory and security forms. In this case the problem can become more acute when doctors complain that they are doing work that could be done by people without their specialist knowledge, and are told by the managers of the hospital or trust that such people are not in the budget, cost too much and, would you believe, are not very productive.

Drucker in the *Harvard Business Review*, Nov–Dec 1995, explains the impact of this ancillary work on nurses in his article "This is Not Job Enrichment":

"This is not job enrichment; it is job impoverishment. It destroys productivity. It saps motivation and morale. Nurses, every attitude survey shows, bitterly resent not being able to spend more time caring for patients. They also believe, understandably, that they are grossly underpaid for what they are capable of doing, while the hospital administrator, equally understandably, believes that they are grossly overpaid for the unskilled work they are actually doing."

The authors go on to quote Robert Zemsky, professor of education at the University of Pennsylvania who has studied the relationship between education and productivity at more than 3000 American workplaces. He reported that on average a 10% increase in workforce educational level led to a hike in productivity of 8.6% measured in a relevant way. He contrasted this with the 3.4% average rise in productivity achieved by a 10% rise in the value of capital equipment. It all goes to show that assets are people, not things. However, Zemsky emphasizes that education does not work on its own, and that it is a combination of investment in T&D and in capital equipment that produces the best productivity results.

Jeffrey Pfeffer, *Achieving Competitive Success Through People*, Harvard Business School Press, 1994

This book sums up the team-based approach that enables leaders to inspire their teams to service the customer better and better and achieve competitive edge:

> "Achieving competitive success through people involves fundamentally altering how we think about the workforce and the employment relationship. It means achieving success by working with people, not by replacing them or limiting the scope of their activities. It entails seeing the workforce as a source of competitive advantage, not just as a cost to be minimized or avoided."

William C. Byham, PhD with Jeff Cox, *Zapp! The Lightning of Empowerment*, reissued revised edition, Century, 1999

A very easy read. Approach it with an open mind and read a fable of effective supervision, leadership, training, and development, integrating an organization's systems and people to improve performance.

WEBSITES

There are many Web-based resources catering for training and development interests. Here are three that have a direct bearing on managing the T&D budget.

Harvard Business Review

Link: www.hbr.org

This is the main site for all the various articles and other products that Harvard Business School and *Harvard Business Review* publish. It includes a forum that readers can join and discuss the articles with other readers and, perhaps more importantly, the authors of the materials. As authors ourselves we are well aware of the usefulness of feedback from readers. Most authors share this opinion and do take part in exploring work that they have written further in forums with readers.

Personneltoday

Link: www.personneltoday.com

Personneltoday has a lot of numerical information, including two sections within its Yardstick section on indicators and benchmarks. Here are two examples of what you will find there.

Seniority affects cost of training. The cost of using external training varies according to the seniority of the employees being trained, a survey by the CIPD (Chartered Institute of Personnel and Development) reveals. Training and Development 2002 surveyed 502 training managers and directors drawn from the CIPD membership nationwide.

While the payments made to training providers vary between companies and regions, directors and senior management training costs an average of £928, the survey claims. This is over £500 a day more than manual workers and £300 more than technicians, supervisors, and clerical/administrative staff. The only group where training costs were found to approach those of senior executive staff were junior managers, the survey finds.

Benchmarking. HR Benchmarker is a paper-based report service offered to PersonnelToday.com users by the MCG Consulting Group. The reports allow you to compare your HR department's performance in areas such as training costs and absenteeism levels against national and sector averages.

Institute of IT Training

Link: www.iitt.org.uk

Since a significant part of most managers' budgets is for IT, this is a useful site for information on all aspects of IT training. Here is their charter.

The Institute of IT Training is a not for profit organisation and is governed by a Board of officials that has statutory responsibility for running the Institute's affairs. These officials include the Chief Executive, Professional Services Director, Company Secretary and two non-executive directors. The Policy Advisory Board (PAB) is the prime communication channel between the Institute's officials and the membership. The PAB, reporting to the main Board, comprises elected chairs of the five Institute committees, together with officials of the Institute.

Institute committees – aims, remit and terms of reference

The Institute runs five separate committees that comprise elected members whose primary purpose is to provide a two-way communication between the Institute Policy Advisory Board and individual members.

The five committees are:

Corporate Committee

Regional Groups Committee

Training Providers Committee

Education Committee

Freelance Committee

The remit and terms of reference of each committee are as follows:

To provide the members it represents with a forum to influence the policy and strategy of the Institute of IT Training

To provide a two-way communication between members and the Institute of IT Training

To act in the best interests of the members it represents.

MAGAZINE

't' magazine

Link: www.tmag.co.uk

This magazine claims to be at the cutting edge of learning, individual development, and the future of work as we move into the twenty-first century. It is published monthly (10 issues per annum), costs just £99.95 and is only available by subscription.

Its strapline, which gives it its relevance to our topic, is "Linking training, education and employment." Here are some examples of what you will find in the magazine and on the site.

Blended learning in financial services institutions. A case study of one firm's approach to using a variety of learning methods to help clients meet learning objectives, by Pete Fullard of Fullard Learning Ltd.

How is work-based learning underperforming? Simon Shaw looks at the apparent underperformance of work-based learning providers, and investigates the underlying reasons, some of which are outside providers' control.

Management development: a perspective from employers. Alison Carter of IES reports on some interesting insights into the challenge facing management development in the UK.

ARTICLES

Of the many articles on the topic we have picked out three (including two from the *Harvard Business Review*).

Daniel Goleman, "Leadership that Gets Results," *Harvard Business Review*, March–April 2000

"New research suggests that the most effective executives use a collection of distinct leadership styles – each in the right measure, at just the right time. Such flexibility is tough to put into action, but it pays off in performance. **And better yet, it can be learned**." (Our emphasis.)

Goleman goes on to look at what these styles are – coercive, authoritative, affiliative, democratic, pacesetting, and coaching. He proposes that the styles taken individually do have a direct and unique impact on the environment that teams and organizations work in, and that this can be clearly seen coming through into performance.

He then introduces us to "Emotional Intelligence," which is "*the ability to manage ourselves and our relationships effectively*" and describes the competencies involved in developing the ability to operate in any of the six leadership styles. Improving emotional intelligence, Goleman maintains, takes months rather than days because it involves not only the thinking part of the brain that masters technical skills and gains knowledge very quickly, but also the emotional centers of the brain. We are, if you like, suppressing our intuitive feelings.

You need a coach over a period of time to help you to unlearn old habits, identify when and why you resort back to the old ways, and plan how to deal with a similar set of circumstances the next time you meet them. He advocates a blended training solution to gaps in leadership techniques, combining classroom work with self-development, coaching, and mentoring on the job.

Of great interest here is the research showing the linkage between a "soft or intangible behavior, leadership style," and the financial performance of an organization.

Professor Edgar Schein, "The Anxiety of Learning," *Harvard Business Review*, March 2002

This looks at the pain of learning and the people that resist what an organization wants of them. It also reminds us that there can be a risk in calculating and monitoring RoI in T&D – people are individual autonomous human beings, and cannot be treated as numbers in a profit and loss account.

John Anderson, "Giving and Receiving Feedback," extracted from *Managing Behavior in Organizations*, by Leonard A. Schlesinger, Robert G. Eccles, & John J. Gabrro, copyright 1983, McGraw-Hill, Inc.

"The chapter discusses a few considerations involved in telling other people how you feel about them especially in a team – 'how to do it' considerations that are apt to be important, if your objective is to help someone become a more effective person, and also to arrive at a more effective interpersonal relationship."

The chapter focuses on feedback in a team environment, but its discussion is equally valid for one-to-one feedback.

Messages: there are tests to apply to ensure feedback should be given. The first – that it is intended to be helpful to the recipient, rather than for the giver of feedback's benefit. To be helpful, three things are necessary.

1 The other person must *understand* what has been said.
2 They must be willing and able to accept it.
3 Both parties must be *able* to do something about it if they choose to.

The chapter covers how to achieve understanding, through being specific and providing recent examples of behavior. It gives guidance on gaining acceptance through:

» establishing a minimum foundation of trust;
» being careful about the style with which feedback is given;
» being descriptive rather than judgmental;
» choosing the right time; and
» appreciating the value of giving some feedback in a team so that it can be checked out.

How to assess the receiver's ability to use feedback through:

» consciously thinking about the issue you wish to provide feedback on; and
» being specific and selecting what is of use.

How to receive feedback through:

» making a sincere effort not to be defensive;
» exploring examples where you do not fully understand;
» summarizing to ensure you fully understand;
» exploring how you feel about the behavior performance issue being fed back; and
» remembering you have rights to accept and reject – feedback is information, that is all.

Ten Steps to Managing Training and Development Finance

Finance is only one element of the training and development plan. Get it into the context of your and the organization's plan by going through these ten steps.

1 Clarify the organization's strategy.
2 Set the objectives and strategy for your team.
3 Define the leadership and culture of your team in the light of your objectives.
4 Examine the core skills and knowledge your team will need to deliver these objectives, including expected behaviors and teamwork.
5 Review the knowledge, processes, and skills of the people required to deliver the plan once again, including expected behaviors and teamwork.
6 Compare the capability requirement with the actual capabilities of the team.

7 Estimate what development interventions you need to fill the gaps and cost them out.

8 Plan and get agreement to a realistic and cost-justified budget.

9 In the appraisal and development planning process, schedule the interventions and decide how to manage each individual.

10 Implement the business plan and monitor the development plans.

1. CLARIFY THE ORGANIZATION'S STRATEGY

It is logically quite impossible to ensure that you are producing good value-for-money training plans unless they contribute to your achieving your objectives, and unless your objectives contribute to the aims and aspirations of your organization. Start, therefore, from your organization's aims. Many organizations put their statement of intent in prominent positions on notice boards and, of course, in their annual report. It is a key purpose-and-strategy statement. They tend now to be getting shorter, and more useful. The old "mission" statement tends to be more motherhood as "To be the best . . .," and therefore much less useful to managers lower down the organization. You should study the senior manager's purpose and use it to understand the validity of your role in it. Every strategy statement and plan for the future should echo this statement of purpose.

Here is an example of a statement of purpose for a health trust with financial problems. It uses a timescale to emphasize the importance of getting through the financial difficulties:

Our purpose, for the period of the next two years, is to ensure that our current service provision to service users and carers across our catchment area is:

» safe and at an appropriate quality level for today
» improved, where it is not safe and at the right quality level, and practice/service change is feasible without additional resource
» delivered within our resource allocation from commissioners.

An equally valid generic health trust one, without such big financial pressures, might read:

Our purpose is to ensure that our current health service provision to service users and carers across our catchment area is:

» excellent quality for today
» improved where it is not, and practice/service change is feasible through additional investment
» delivered within our resource allocation from commissioners (on behalf of the taxpayer).

It is easy to see how the differences that these two similar statements of purposes would make to the T&D plan. It is plain in the first that any additional expenditure on T&D will have to be met by a reduction in costs somewhere else in the organization. In the second one, however, if a manager can make a compelling business case, they may well be able to increase their spend.

Now, the detection of the overall strategy should not be too difficult. After all, the board of an organization is responsible for analyzing possible future plans, deciding on the appropriate strategy, and then communicating this to all the people who will be involved in its execution. Those involved in the execution are staff at all levels and in all functions. It is necessary that a consistent pyramid of plans ensures that what is happening on the shop floor and at the point of sale and delivery fits in with the plans of the directors. This communication is very difficult to get right, and its failure is obvious to staff and customers alike.

If the communication of this strategy in your organization is unclear, or stated in terms that do not make it easy to understand your part in it, you need a simple technique for detecting and documenting the board's strategy. Do this by means of the organization activity matrix, Table 10.1. Published material will contain in some form, statements of the organization's products and markets' segmentation, and you should be able to reproduce this in a simple matrix, perhaps confining yourself to the product market segments that involve your team. The harder this exercise is to do, the less well is the board explaining itself, probably to shareholders and staff alike.

In non-profitmaking organizations this exercise may need some creative thought. But in the end every team and every job has a product or service to supply to an internal or external market (see Table 10.1).

2. SET THE OBJECTIVES AND STRATEGY FOR YOUR TEAM

The aim of this step is to produce a set of objectives so that the requirements that you will place on your team are clear and well understood. If you and/or they do not know what is required it is impossible to know whether you are likely to do a good or a bad job. You will have to break these down into the performance requirements

Table 10.1 The activity matrix.

Activity matrix	Market 1	Market 2	Market 3	Market 4	Market 5	Market 6	Market 7	Market 8
Product/service 1								
Product/service 2								
Product/service 3								
Product/service 4								
Product/service 5								

for each individual by defining their objectives. This forms the starting point. The strategy records how you are going to go about this.

Here is an example of an objective for an organization whose internal customers are the divisional management teams of a large multinational:

> Within eighteen months to have held a joint planning session with at least two divisional management teams and the corporate and policy resources committee.

Make sure the objectives are SMART – Stretching, Measurable, Achievable, Related to your customer, and Time-targeted. The strength of these objectives will be tested when it comes to asking for resources and money for development programs, so get them right.

It is very useful then to add a strategy statement of your own to show how you are going to achieve this. This helps to expose gaps in the skills and competencies of the team in trying to achieve the objectives. Here is one possible strategy statement for the above objective:

> We shall achieve this level of partnership by emphasizing at all times our high profile in the company, and our knowledge of many internal divisions and external companies getting benefits out of our products and services.

3. DEFINE THE LEADERSHIP AND CULTURE OF YOUR TEAM IN THE LIGHT OF YOUR OBJECTIVES

Now sit back and think about your team and how it goes about its business. Does it have the leadership and culture necessary for you to achieve your objectives? Suppose you are frequently faced with the following problem.

Your team leaders sit on a problem even for a short time, maybe two weeks, more than they should. Perhaps they are involved with other teams who live in a heavy blame culture. When the delay becomes long and you get involved, how supportive are you? Are you confident enough to absorb failure – to tell your bosses that something has gone wrong and to be positive in helping your team leaders to sort it all out? If you have got this right, well done; now think about how good your team is at it. If you need to work in this area you need a plan for change. This should be your first priority before moving into major development of the team or individuals within it.

» State the need in a simple sentence such as "We need to remove people's fear of blame in order to encourage them to be very open about their performance and skills and knowledge problems."
» Set the priority for this need for change by considering the impact and urgency of it. You can probably only tackle those with high impact and high urgency.
» Work out an action plan to make this change and put the budget for these activities down as a priority for the overall training budget before you consider individual needs. This step, if you like, addresses the environment the team needs to work in, in order to deliver your objectives.

4. EXAMINE THE CORE SKILLS YOUR TEAM WILL NEED TO DELIVER THESE OBJECTIVES

Managers tend to use hunch and instinct in this area, but will normally benefit from a more analytical approach. Against each team objective consider three areas of capability.

» Knowledge of content – what technical, professional knowledge, and qualifications are needed to be able to perform well?
» Processes – what defined processes, such as project management, will the team need?
» Skills – look across the whole spectrum of personal, relationship, and management skills.

5. REVIEW THE KNOWLEDGE, PROCESSES, AND SKILLS OF THE PEOPLE REQUIRED TO DELIVER THE PLAN

For each job or role in your team there will be an ideal profile against these capabilities; so complete the analysis by categorizing the levels of capability required. Remember at this stage to do it by role, not by person. If you have your people in mind too early you will not produce an objective statement of their requirements, and it will cloud your judgment. An effective way of documenting this analysis is a four-point method as follows:

» N/A – no capability required for this knowledge, process or skill area;
» L – low level required, perhaps simply the awareness that the capability is required in a process in which they are involved, but they at this stage do not need to have it themselves;
» M – medium level needed; they are competent to perform this part of the role without any need for supervision; and
» H – high level of expertise required, so such people can teach others and improve the job, or the processes within the job where such opportunities exist, without being instructed.

Think in teams. One of the points of working in teams is that not everyone needs the same level of capability; so do not assume that when you are defining capabilities by role.

6. COMPARE THE CAPABILITY REQUIREMENT WITH THE ACTUAL CAPABILITIES OF THE TEAM

The starting point for building capabilities is to define the gap between the level the person is at, and what is required to make them successful in their current role, and in future roles. This should be quite straightforward to document if you have done the preceding analysis thoroughly. Money, never far away in a plan of this kind, starts to come to the fore here. Unless you are very lucky, some gaps will be large and expensive to close. Look at the impact and urgency of the gaps and give high-impact, high-urgency gaps a priority for attention. Incidentally, as you go through two or three iterations of this process, you should find that the urgency of closing the gap will decrease. If every gap is going to have a huge impact on performance in the short term, high impact, and high urgency, you are basically firefighting. In an ideal world your training and development budget would be spent anticipating requirements, which means working on gaps that are still high-impact, perhaps, but lower urgency so that you have time to address the problem.

7. ESTIMATE WHAT DEVELOPMENT INTERVENTIONS YOU NEED TO FILL THE GAPS AND COST THEM OUT

There are many ways of closing the gaps. Training, using internal or external resources, self-development, mentoring secondment, and so on, in any variety of combination will do the job. Think as broadly as possible so that you opt for cheaper ways of doing things that are equally valid in closing the gaps. Progress may depend on the availability of specialists and mentors.

Incidentally, be very careful when using mentors. A mentor may not need to be expert to do the mentoring job, but they must be competent. Someone who is only aware of how the skill is carried out may do more harm than good if you allow them to mentor others.

Increasingly, managers are using technology to improve the cost-effectiveness of training – see Chapter 4 (The E-Dimension).

At the end of this step you should have a matrix with your people down the left-hand side, capabilities across the top, and a description of the development intervention you plan for them, along with its cost. Table 10.2 is an example of this. Add it up and you have the next challenge – selling it to your boss and getting the money.

8. PLAN AND GET AGREEMENT TO A REALISTIC AND COST-JUSTIFIED BUDGET

Just before you start this step, try not to get hung up on the money side of all this. Remember, that if the result of the above seven steps is a strong business case linking the training and development plan directly to the performance of individuals, and then to the performance of the team, you have earned the budget and will get it on merit. A lot of managers, even senior ones, do actually listen to reason – honestly.

In Chapter 6 and Chapter 7 we discuss the state of the art in this, and give some examples of what people have done to produce well-justified training budget submissions.

The presentation of your budget submission is best seen as a contract between two parties – your team and the organization. From a good analysis of the strengths, weaknesses, opportunities, and threats, you have produced a series of business objectives. You have made sure they

Table 10.2 The individual/capability matrix.

Capability	Whole team	Team member A	Team member B	Team member C
Personal leadership and development			Specialist external coach – 4 sessions £250 per session	
Team-working	Facilitated team development program – 4 workshops throughout the year £7,000			
Meetings management		Internal training course – £200		
Presentation skills				Internal training course – £300
Increased understanding of business partners				Shadowing in a key partner organization – no additional cost

are SMART, so you will be able to demonstrate just how stretching they are. (Do not expect a willing audience to a request for training budget in order to achieve a simple set of objectives that would probably be achieved even if the whole team went off on a bicycling tour of the Scottish Highlands.)

But back to the contract – you are basically saying that you will achieve these objectives in the short term, and be in a position to do even better in the long term, if your managers will give this amount of money to spend on T&D. You may have to compromise a bit, so build that into your plans as you do in any other negotiation, but do not give way on the main principle. You have to be prepared to say that you will have to adjust your objectives down the way if management cannot find the will or the money to fund the development plan. This does not mean that you should be inflexible. After all, because they look at the plans of so many teams, managers, particularly senior ones, can make useful contributions on alternative ways to achieve the same thing.

Remember that we do not live in an ideal world. Beware of the management team that naturally agrees to your part of the contract, the achievement of the business objectives, but declines to give you the resources you need to implement the plan. If this is your situation use the time before you present the final budget to soften up as many of the management team as you can.

9. IN THE APPRAISAL AND DEVELOPMENT PLANNING PROCESS, SCHEDULE THE INTERVENTIONS AND DECIDE HOW TO MANAGE EACH INDIVIDUAL

Before setting out on this step, take a moment to consider how much you want the team to conform to the behavior you have in mind, and how much you want to encourage individualism. Any planner will tell you that in a team planning session the most unlikely people come up with insights that the rest of the team has missed, perhaps because they find it difficult to believe that something they have been doing for years could be improved by change. Diversity of style and behavior, therefore, is important to the dynamics of a team and to its ability in the words of the politicians "to think the unthinkable." Take care not to use the T&D budget to produce clones of you. It will not work, and anyway, you are not a deity.

Look also at how different people respond to your natural style of management. Fiona has been in situations that looked on the face of it beyond repair, and dismissal seemed the only option; but has, after hard experience, turned them round simply by reflecting and learning herself, and adjusting her natural style. Intuitively, given a critical problem, Fiona knows that she will go into directive mode until the problem is solved, and the team can go back to normal delegation. Some people, however, require a much more social approach, where their supervisor listens to their problems (and believe us, this can be a long listen); sympathize, and then assist as well as guide them to find the way out of the business problem.

Take this into account before you schedule training and development. Everybody in an organization wants to know where they stand and how their manager views the way they are doing their job. They want continuous feedback whether it is positive or negative. Give your successful achievers feedback to help them sustain their performance. Use feedback for others in the team to identify the skills, knowledge, and attitude they need to improve the way they are working. Don't forget to praise good performance whenever you see it – people like to be told that they are achieving high standards. Praise keeps them doing the right things and encourages them to do even better. Working like this means that you do not store up any concerns that you have about people, and that there are no surprises when you come to the formal appraisal review.

There are two parts to the formal appraisal. The first part is the performance review, where you and the appraisee agree how well they have achieved their objectives, and developed their skills and knowledge during the period under review. The second part is the developmental review, during which the manager and the appraisee discuss and agree what they need to do in the future to sustain the process of achieving objectives. The developmental review aims at continuously improving the appraisee's capabilities and preparing them to take on more responsibilities or a more senior role. Do the two parts together to emphasize the link between them.

10. IMPLEMENT THE BUSINESS PLAN AND MONITOR THE DEVELOPMENT PLANS

Just as there is a strong link between the strategy and objectives of teams in an organization, so there is a connected set of training plans. At every regular review session you need to review the individual's training and development plan. That way you maintain the match between the needs of an individual, the needs of the team they are working in, and the organization as a whole. The appraisal and each individual development plan are important sources of information for the organization to plan its overall training requirements, and to use economies of scale to make the training budget as effective as possible. Make your development plans and the results you want to achieve as specific as possible to assist in this process. This will ensure that all the people in the organization are developing in a way that helps them to achieve their objectives.

Frequently Asked Questions (FAQs)

Q1: Do you know how to get your training and development budget into the context of your organization's objectives?

A: See Chapter 10.

Q2: Do you have a model for planning and allocating resources to training and development?

A: See Chapter 6.

Q3: Is there an electronic template for assessing return on investment?

A: See Chapter 6.

Q4: Can I define the leadership and culture of our team in the light of our objectives?

A: See Chapter 10.

Q5: How can I know how to measure the productivity of knowledge workers?

A: See Chapter 9.

Q6: Can I compare the productivity hike gained from education with that gained by capital investment?

A: See Chapter 9.

Q7: Can I find how overheads added to internal profit and loss accounts can distort cost-benefit exercises entirely?

A: See Chapter 8.

Q8: Can I maintain the centralize/decentralize argument in T&D planning?

A: See Chapter 5.

Q9: Can I describe the different way that individuals learn?

A: See Chapter 2.

Q10: Do I have access to tools to help keep my training and development financial thinking and skills up-to-date on a regular basis?

A: See Chapter 10.

Index

EXPRESSEXEC – BUSINESS THINKING AT YOUR FINGERTIPS

ExpressExec is a 12-module resource with 10 titles in each module. Combined they form a complete resource of current business practice. Each title enables the reader to quickly understand the key concepts and models driving management thinking today.

Innovation

01.01 *Innovation Express*
01.02 *Global Innovation*
01.03 *E-Innovation*
01.04 *Creativity*
01.05 *Technology Leaders*
01.06 *Intellectual Capital*
01.07 *The Innovative Individual*
01.08 *Taking Ideas to Market*
01.09 *Creating an Innovative Culture*
01.10 *Managing Intellectual Property*

Enterprise

02.01 *Enterprise Express*
02.02 *Going Global*
02.03 *E-Business*
02.04 *Corporate Venturing*
02.05 *Angel Capital*
02.06 *Managing Growth*
02.07 *Exit Strategies*
02.08 *The Entrepreneurial Individual*
02.09 *Business Planning*
02.10 *Creating the Entrepreneurial Organization*

Strategy

03.01 *Strategy Express*
03.02 *Global Strategy*
03.03 *E-Strategy*
03.04 *The Vision Thing*
03.05 *Strategies for Hypergrowth*
03.06 *Complexity and Paradox*
03.07 *The New Corporate Strategy*
03.08 *Balanced Scorecard*
03.09 *Competitive Intelligence*
03.10 *Future Proofing*

Marketing

04.01 *Marketing Express*
04.02 *Global Marketing*
04.03 *E-Marketing*
04.04 *Customer Relationship Management*
04.05 *Reputation Management*
04.06 *Sales Promotion*
04.07 *Channel Management*
04.08 *Branding*
04.09 *Market Research*
04.10 *Sales Management*

Finance

05.01 *Finance Express*
05.02 *Global Finance*
05.03 *E-Finance*
05.04 *Investment Appraisal*
05.05 *Understanding Accounts*
05.06 *Shareholder Value*
05.07 *Valuation*
05.08 *Strategic Cash Flow Management*
05.09 *Mergers and Acquisitions*
05.10 *Risk Management*

Operations and Technology

06.01 *Operations and Technology Express*
06.02 *Operating Globally*
06.03 *E-Processes*
06.04 *Supply Chain Management*
06.05 *Crisis Management*
06.06 *Project Management*
06.07 *Managing Quality*
06.08 *Managing Technology*
06.09 *Measurement and Internal Audit*
06.10 *Making Partnerships Work*

Available from:
www.expressexec.com

Customer Service Department
John Wiley & Sons Ltd
Southern Cross Trading Estate
1 Oldlands Way, Bognor Regis
West Sussex, PO22 9SA
Tel: +44(0)1243 843 294
Fax: +44(0)1243 843 303
Email: cs-books@wiley.co.uk

Printed and bound by CPI Group (UK) Ltd, Croydon, CR0 4YY

13/04/2025

14656559-0003